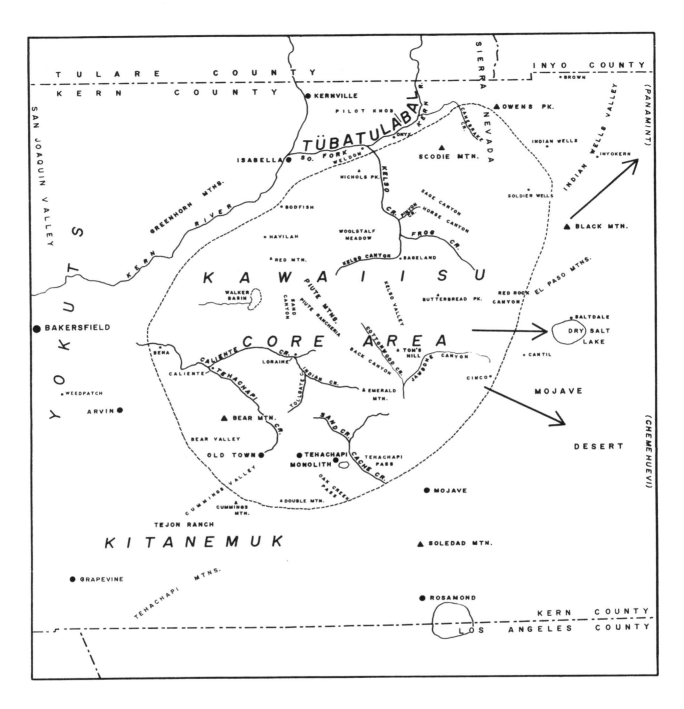

TULARE   COUNTY

KERN   COUNTY

INYO   COUNTY

● BROWN

SAN JOAQUIN VALLEY

● KERNVILLE

PILOT KNOB

SIERRA   NEVADA

▲ OWENS PK.

(PANAMINT)

TÜBATULABAL

CANEBRAKE CR.

KERN R.

ONYX

INDIAN WELLS

ISABELLA ●   SO. FORK   WELDON

NICHOLS PK.

▲ SCODIE MTN.

SOLDIER WELLS ●

INYOKERN

INDIAN WELLS VALLEY

GREENHORN MTNS.

● BODFISH

KELSO CR.

SAGE CANYON

PINION CR.

HORSE CANYON

KERN   RIVER

● HAVILAH

WOOLSTALF MEADOW

FROG   CR.

▲ BLACK MTN.

Y O K U T S

▲ RED MTN.

KELSO CANYON

SAGELAND

K A W A I I S U

WALKER BASIN

PIUTE MTNS.

SAND CANYON

KELSO VALLEY

BUTTERBREAD PK. ●

RED ROCK CANYON

EL PASO MTNS.

● SALTDALE

● BAKERSFIELD

C O R E   A R E A

PIUTE RANCHERIA

COTTONWOOD CR.

▲ TOM'S HILL

BACK CANYON

JAWBONE CANYON

● CANTIL

DRY SALT LAKE

BENA

CALIENTE CR.

LORAINE

TEHACHAPI

INDIAN CR.

● WEEDPATCH

CALIENTE

TOLLGATE CR.

▲ EMERALD MTN.

CINCO ●

M O J A V E

ARVIN ●

▲ BEAR MTN.

BEAR MTN. CR.

SAND CR.

D E S E R T

BEAR VALLEY

OLD TOWN ●

● TEHACHAPI

MONOLITH ●

CACHE CR.

TEHACHAPI PASS

OAK CREEK PASS

(CHEMEHUEVI)

CUMMINGS VALLEY

▲ DOUBLE MTN.

● MOJAVE

▲ CUMMINGS MTN.

TEJON RANCH

K I T A N E M U K

▲ SOLEDAD MTN.

● GRAPEVINE

TEHACHAPI MTNS.

● ROSAMOND

KERN   COUNTY

LOS   ANGELES   COUNTY

CALIF.

N

S E A S O N A L   T R I P S

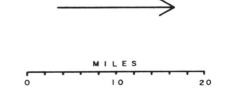

MILES

0   10   20

Ballena Press Anthropological Papers No. 18
Series Editors: Lowell John Bean and Thomas C. Blackburn

KAWAIISU MYTHOLOGY

An Oral Tradition of South-Central California

by

Maurice L. Zigmond, Ph.D.
Honorary Research Associate, Harvard Universtiy

A BALLENA PRESS PUBLICATION

Ballena Press Anthropological Papers Editors:

Thomas C. Blackburn
Lowell John Bean

ISBN 0-87919-089-2

Ballena Press
823 Valparaiso Avenue
Menlo Park, CA 94025

Orders:

Ballena Press Publishers Services
P.O. Box 2510
Novato, CA 94948
Phone (415) 883-3530; Fax (415) 883-4280

Printed in the United States of America.
Second Printing.

Contents

Illustrations

Cover: Emma Williams with some of her baskets, 1936.

Frontispiece: Map of Kawaiisu territory, drawn by Larry Eckhart.

1. a. (1.-r.) Gladys Nichols, Lizzie Nichols, Emma Williams,
      Sophie Williams, and Elsie Williams, 1936.
   b. Emma Williams and Maurice Zigmond, 1936.

2. a. Sadie Williams, daughter of Emma Williams, 1937.
   b. Kawaiisu women pruning wild tobacco, 1937.

3. a. John Nichols with his hand in a mortar-hole, 1937.
   b. John and Louisa Marcus at home in Monolith, 1937.

4. a. Refugia Williams and daughters, 1937.
   b. Sam Willie and his family at Monolith, 1937.

5. a. Charley Haslem in Kelso Valley, 1936.
   b. Bob Rabbit, Kawaiisu weather shaman, 1936.

6. a. Setimo Girado, 1937.
   b. Gladys Nichols Girado, 1973.

7. a. (1.-r.) Lida Girado and Clara Girado Williams, 1973.
   b. Bertha Willie Goings at Tehachapi, 1973.

8. a. Martina Collins in front of brush shade, 1936.
   b. Ramona Greene and her children, 1936 or 1937.

9. a. Marcelino Rivera and Isabelle Gonzales at Tejon, 1937.
   b. (1.-r.) Maurice Zigmond and Stephen Cappannari at Cape
      Cod, 1948.

10. a. Johnnie Shoshone on the ridge of the Panamint Range, 1938.
    b. Andy Shoshone and his grandfather, Panamint George, 1938.

Foreword

     Maurice L. Zigmond's *Kawaiisu Mythology* is a major contribution to the ethnographic literature concerned with Native American societies, and one, moreover, of superior literary quality. It represents the culmination of nearly four decades of research carried out by three different scholars (two of whom are now deceased) in an important but poorly described area of California. It is also the first publication of monograph length on the Kawaiisu, a hitherto obscure and little-known tribal group for which only sparse data were previously available.

     For many years, a hiatus in significant ethnographic research has existed in California, a hiatus that is now ending as previously unstudied groups are beginning to receive some attention. Major bodies of data generated in the past by such scholars as J. P. Harrington and C. W. Merriam are being exhumed and published by younger anthropologists; in addition, already-published data are being reexamined and compared in terms of new perspectives and theoretical models. The present monograph is unusual in that it involves elements of both--an older scholar, after many years devoted to other issues, here reexamines and analyzes his own (and others') previously unpublished data, and in so doing adds a fascinating personal dimension to an already significant contribution.

     In an excellent introductory essay, Zigmond provides the reader with a history of ethnographic research on the Kawaiisu, and with comparative observations on the mythology of other ethnic groups in Southern California and the Great Basin. The editors are particularly impressed by the numerous similarities in both content and style between the oral tradition presented here and those with which we are personally familiar; for example, many of the existential and normative postulates that are present in Cahuilla, Chumash, and Kitanemuk oral traditions are also evident in the Kawaiisu stories, albeit in different structural frames and with significant ethnic idiosyncrasies. The appearance of this new corpus of narratives will hopefully tempt scholars to reevaluate broader aspects of Native American oral traditions in south-central California and the Southwest.

     As might be expected, particularly close parallels exist between Kawaiisu oral narratives and those of the Chemehuevi, a group that has also been rescued from obscurity in the last several years through the efforts of another senior scholar, Carobeth Laird. Laird, former wife of ethnologist John P. Harrington and widow of Harrington's Chemehuevi informant George

Laird, has already published a great deal of information on Chemehuevi myths, although her definitive study *Mirror and Pattern: George Laird's World of Chemehuevi Mythology* (Malki Museum Press) has not yet appeared. Zigmond draws upon Laird's contributions and details the many striking similarities that exist between the two traditions. Analogous comparisons of these two bodies of data with others now available are very much in order.

Zigmond touches upon many fascinating topics and raises a number of significant issues in his introductory essay. He sets the coyote cycle in an interesting perspective; discusses the mythological age, magical transformation, visits to the underworld, and the natural hierarchy of the plant and animal world; explores the topic of narrative types; and details explanations of various natural phenomena. A considerable amount of useful ethnographic and ethnobotanical lore is present in these narratives as well; for example, it is interesting to note that the characters in the myths speak a variety of languages, just as people did in ethnographic times. In addition, there is significant information on behavior and ethics, and on myth in the context of culture change. As Zigmond notes, the narratives often take various exogenous phenomena into account--thus the existence of different racial types, for example, is readily integrated with the traditional lore. Unfortunately, songs (which were frequently associated with the narratives) were not recorded; however, further work with the John P. Harrington collections may once again provide us with future insights into the musical traditions of the area and their relationship to the oral traditions--Gary Tegler's work with Chumash music is an example of what may be done along these lines. In short, the present monograph is an exceptionally valuable addition to the anthropological literature on Native Americans, and one which we take great pleasure in commending to the reader.

Lowell John Bean
Thomas Blackburn

Introduction

During the long nights of winter, one may imagine that in "old times" a Kawaiisu family and perhaps a few neighbors would gather around the fire and listen to the older people tell stories which they had heard before and would hear again. If the men (not the women) were smoking cane "pipes," they would soon fall asleep, since it was said that three puffs of the strong native tobacco were about all one could take in an evening. (The pipe could be snuffed out in the sandy soil and used again.) Winter was the proper time for the telling of tales. The usual explanation is that at other seasons the narrator (and perhaps the listeners, too) were vulnerable to being bitten by rattlesnakes. The same motive is given for the custom of jumping into cold water the next morning: snakes are reputed to stay away from water except in September (Zigmond 1977:91).

Such considerations did not deter three of us, quite independently, from recording Kawaiisu myths, as well as other cultural data, in partial fulfillment of requirements for Ph.D. degrees in anthropology. Circumstances made it necessary for us to schedule our ethnographic visits in the summers and, while consultants might occasionally indicate that this was not the proper season for story-telling, they usually yielded to our request. For all of us, the gathering of myths was but one aspect of our ethnographic concerns. Theodore D. McCown, whose contact with the tribe was apparently limited to a brief trip in 1929, has nineteen stories in his field-notes, according to my count. Unaware of McCown's activities, I made my own first visit to the Kawaiisu in the summer of 1936 and during four successive summers thereafter. I returned for brief periods several times in the 1970s. In all I recorded sixty-seven myths. For three summers (1947-1949), Stephen C. Cappannari--like McCown from the University of California at Berkeley (I was associated with Yale University)--collected a total of fifty-six tales. Both McCown and Cappannari died without publishing their materials. While nothing came of the idea, Cappannari and I at one time had thought of preparing jointly a volume of Kawaiisu stories for children. He submitted a sample manuscript to at least two publishers under the title *Coyote Tales of California Indians*. I saw one response expressing "interest," but the project went no further.

During the summers of 1937 and 1938, in the course of my ethnographic fieldwork with the Kawaiisu, I made two quick forays into the surrounding area to locate, if possible, survivors of two neighboring tribes. An extended study of the native culture was not feasible, but I was primarily

9

interested in finding people with knowledge of ethnobotanical traditions.
I was accompanied in 1938 by Noel Wallace, a botanical student at Claremont
College.

A short trip southward brought me to the great Tejon Ranch, in the
midst of which was a small community of ranch workers and their families.
Here I found two elderly people, Marcelino Rivera and Isabella Gonzales,
brother and sister, whose usual speech was Spanish but who remembered an
Indian language which proved to be Kitanemuk. In the process of obtaining
from them the names and usages of wild plants, I recorded such other cultural data as they could recall. These included two myths which have been
added to the present collection. One of these tales, which I have called
"Coyote Kidnaps Mountain Lion's Sons", was published thirty years before by
Kroeber (1907:243-4). He calls it "The Panther's Children and Coyote," and
states that it is a "Gitanemuk Shoshonean" myth told to him by a "Yauelmani
Yokuts." The similarity between Kroeber's version and mine is obvious.

The other native people from whom I sought ethnobotanical information were the Panamint, also known as the Koso or Western Shoshone, whose
habitat was to the northeast of the central Kawaiisu area. I drove to within
a quarter mile of the ridge of the Panamint Range. By standing on the ridge
itself, it is possible to see the highest and lowest points in the contiguous
forty-eight states: Mt. Whitney and Death Valley. Nearby I located an
elderly Panamint man, Panamint George, and his grandson, Andy Shoshone. The
latter was helpful in English translation. Aside from ethnobotanical and
other cultural data, they provided me with four Panamint myths, and later
took me to the dwelling of Johnnie Shoshone, a man of about eighty years,
who told me a fifth tale. The five stories have been included here. They
reveal both similarities and differences when compared with analogous Kawaiisu
myths. For example, in "Coyote and His Brother Wolf," the personality of
Coyote contrasts with the usual characterization found in Kawaiisu tales.
The Panamint "Cottontail and the Sun" myth expands the adventures of Cottontail beyond those recounted in the parallel Kawaiisu myth.

When I recently undertook to organize my own data for publication,
it seemed proper that the materials collected by my colleagues ought to be
incorporated and that due credit should be given to them for their contributions. Mrs. McCown and Mrs. Cappannari agreed with this proposal and cooperated
fully. Several papers constructed in this fashion have already appeared,
and others are in process.[1] The integration of the myths revealed many
duplicates; there are now seventy-two different tales represented by one
hundred fifty versions. Several of the stories do not come within the usual
conception of mythology. Thus "A Story of Cannibalism" may reflect an
actual episode; "The Story of *Pogwiti*" may be an historical record; and whatever else "A Gambling Story" may be, it is clearly not an aboriginal Kawaiisu
folktale. Twenty-two myths stand alone; of the remainder, the duplication
varies from two to six, but none can be considered a "carbon copy." There
is diversity in some plot details and (occasionally) in the *dramatis personae*.

---

[1]"The Supernatural World of the Kawaiisu" (in *Flowers of the Wind*,
1977); "Kawaiisu Basketry" (*Journal of California Anthropology*, 1979);
Kawaiisu Ethnobotany (in press); *Kawaiisu Dictionary* (to be published).

Consultants seemed to recall some myths more readily than others. Thus in the combined collection of stories, there are six versions of "Coyote Marries His Daughter," and six (if one counts McCown's three fragments as one) of the tale I have designated "First Food and the Population Problem"; five versions each of "Coyote and the Weather," "The Bears at Walker Basin," "The Race from Victorville to Koso Hot Springs," and the brief and puzzling "Tale of Tobacco"; and four versions each of "Coyote and Mountain Lion" (or Wolf), "Coyote and Pitch," "The Giant Grasshopper," "How the Kawaiisu Got Fire," "How the Kawaiisu Got Pinyons," "The Origin of Deer Hunting," and "A Visit to the Underworld." Of the fourteen consultants who served as narrators, only one told stories to all three of us.

The task of gathering Kawaiisu myths and offering them in English presented the usual problems inherent in such oral transmission. The procedure involved at least two, and often three, participants: the narrator, the translator—if the linguistic facility of the story-teller was limited to his own tongue—and the recorder (anthropologist). Obviously there were personality factors at work at every stage. Sometimes the story-teller was meticulous in setting forth the details of the narrative. But he might be guilty of forgetfulness, carelessness, indifference, or incompetence. Furthermore, adequacy or inadequacy was not necessarily a constant condition. Such temporary states as fatigue or mood played a role. For example, a comparison of the material contributed by two narrators, Santos Phillips and Emma Williams, is instructive. Anna H. Gayton, who published *Areal Affiliations of California Folktales* in 1935, read such myths as I had recorded during my first year in the field and commented, "It appears that you have an excellent story-teller in Emma Williams. . . ." On the other hand, some stories of Santos Phillips, such as "The Bears at Walker Basin" and "The Race Between Frog, Coyote, and the Sun," do not offer a clear account of events. As for the translators, both Elsie Garcia and Sadie Williams rendered Emma Williams' tales in English. There are differences, but they are relatively minor. To make a judgment of the work of the three anthropologists would be unfair, since it is apparent that McCown often took notes in telegraphic style and would surely have revised them if he had gotten around to preparing them for publication. I have the impression that Cappannari sometimes recorded with tongue in cheek.

Overall, the time-span involved in the assembling of this mythological collection has been about forty-five years. Within that period, the stories give evidence of stability, especially if one considers the dwindling population and cultural loss of the tribe. In one instance, a supplemental fact was suggested thirty years after the original telling. On occasion a bystander added a few details without objection from the narrator, who may have forgotten the items or considered them unimportant. The duplication of tales has allowed for a checking of details that otherwise would have been impossible. As presented here, each myth version is introduced with the names of the collector, narrator, and translator—except where this information is not indicated in the fieldnotes.

As already suggested, story-telling among the Kawaiisu was a rather intimate affair. There is no evidence that tales were recounted before sizable gatherings, except perhaps when the recital had some direct

bearing on a special event taking place.[2] Thus a family tradition may have
grown up around the telling of certain myths. If so, this circumstance may
explain the fact that Setimo and Marie Girado (husband and wife), who told
stories to me and to Cappannari, respectively, about ten years apart, related some myth-details which were at variance with the same tales as told
by others. Thus the oft-repeated tale of "Coyote and Mountain Lion" becomes
"Coyote and Wolf" to the Girados. Similarly, in the "Coyote Marries His
Daughter" story, the Girados begin with an episode involving Coyote and his
mother-in-law, and end with the choking of Coyote by his daughters, who fill
his mouth with pounded bunchgrass seed; in Emma Williams' version the
mother-in-law incident is omitted and, while the bunchgrass seed prompts
Coyote to beg for water, his death is due to his yelling for his family to
come back from the sky. Some myths may be conceived of as being comprised of
several independent segments which sometimes are considered separate tales
and at other times regrouped to form another myth. When Emma Williams told
me the "Giant" episodes, she united them into one narrative; to Cappannari
she related them individually. Setimo Girado on one occasion combined three
unrelated events; others presented them as isolated happenings. Again,
Rafael Girado's "First Death" contains elements which are to be found scattered in other stories. The myth "Coyote and Canada Geese" begins distinc-
tively, but concludes with one of the "Coyote Marries His Daughters" endings.
This shifting of mythological materials is not unique to the Kawaiisu. As
Blackburn notes in *December's Child*:

> [A] characteristic of many narratives (and one that is widespread in
> California) is their composite quality: several distinct incidents
> from various sources may be combined to create a new story or used to
> modify or expand an old one. Thus two different narratives may share
> one or more incidents, yet not really be variants of the same story at
> all; or variants of a story can be quite different in certain sections
> . . . [1975:23].

COMPARATIVE NOTES

It is to be expected that myths are subject to the same distributional and diffusionary movements as other culture traits. Mythological
correspondences are to be found in all geographical directions. In 1931,
Henrietta Schmerler identified the tale "Trickster Marries His Daughter" in
twenty-nine tribal traditions west of the Rocky Mountains; since then the
story has been found in additional cultures including that of the Kawaiisu--
where its popularity has already been noted. Gayton (cited above) made
brief comments on the distributional associations of those of my myths she
recognized; I reproduce her comments in the appropriate places in this work.

The Kawaiisu lived aboriginally in South-Central California, an
area of cultural and linguistic diversity. Their language belongs to the
Southern Numic branch of Uto-Aztecan; nearby were several other peoples of

---

[2]The only situation which seemed to fit this latter description
was the drinking of jimsonweed by one or more young people. It was said
that an aged person would talk to them of the Beginnings and of the Four
Medicines. (See *Datura* in the *Kawaiisu Ethnobotany*.)

Uto-Aztecan stock: The Tübatulabal to the north, Southern Californian (Takic) groups to the south, the Panamint (Western Shoshoni) to the north-east, and (separated by the Mohave Desert) the Chemehuevi to the east, also Southern Numic speakers. Only to the west were there non-Uto-Aztecans: the Yokuts, with whom, despite geographical proximity, there were no friendly ties.

When separating the California and Great Basin culture areas, an-thropologists usually put the north-south boundary line along the ridge of the Sierra Nevada mountains. Such a line divides the Kawaiisu territory in two, but it has become customary to consider Kawaiisu culture as belonging basically to the Great Basin.[3] The Tübatulabal, their immediate neighbors to the north, are classified rather arbitrarily as Californian. Gayton (personal communication) notes that the Kawaiisu myths offer "confirmatory evidence of the connection with (Great) Basin rather than San Joaquin (Yokuts) culture." While her general conclusion is valid, it is nonetheless true that there are a few striking Kawaiisu-Yokuts cognates. Similarly, there are some close correspondences between Kawaiisu and Tübatulabal tales, but here the geographical proximity as well as the amicable relations between the two groups leads one to suspect that there may have been some direct borrowing.[4] The relevant myths will be indicated as they occur in this study.

Although no Kawaiisu folktales have previously been published, there exists a considerable body of Great Basin mythology which constitutes a proper framework for the material to be presented here. Ethnographies by Isabel Kelly and Julian Steward, Edward Sapir's Kaibab Ute and Uintah Ute texts,[5] and Robert Lowie's Shoshonean tales (which could have been called Great Basin tales) all include myths that allow detailed comparisons with Kawaiisu myths. In particular, the last-named source contains stories with titles such as "Bungling Host," "Hoodwinked Dancers," "Owl's Wife," and others which suggest Kawaiisu parallels.

Kawaiisu and Chemehuevi

Within the past several years Carobeth Laird, widow of a Chemehuevi Indian, has published a book and a number of papers[6] whose primary focus has been on Chemehuevi mythology. Since this tribe is one of the closest neigh-bors of the Kawaiisu and has a language of the same sub-stock (Southern Numic or, as previously designated in the literature, Ute-Chemehuevi), Laird's work affords an excellent opportunity to compare elements in the folklore of the two peoples. While neither the Kawaiisu nor the Chemehuevi myth corpus

_____

[3]There are, however, some obvious "Californian" traits. Thus the most important vegetal food of the Kawaiisu is the acorn, and their pre-ferred tobacco species is *Nicotiana bigelovii*.

[4]In "The Supernatural World of the Kawaiisu" (Zigmond 1977), reference is made to some resemblances between Kawaiisu and Tübatulabal be-liefs (pp. 74, 80-81). These will not be repeated here.

[5]These texts constitute a section of Sapir's *The Southern Paiute Language* (1930).

[6]See References.

can be considered exhaustive, the number of parallel episodes which emerge is striking. The resultant situation justifies detailed treatment.

It will be noted that the incidents to be cited, though clearly cognate, are often found in contrasting backgrounds and settings. Thus it would appear that the myth elements were transmitted--in either direction-- as individual and perhaps isolated happenings, rather than as segments of an integrated whole. And even though folktales are apt to carry along their own settings in the process of transmission, the distinctive natural and social environment of the host culture is inevitably reflected in the narratives. Thus the Gila monster figures in the Chemehuevi stories but not in those of the Kawaiisu; actually, no Kawaiisu name for the reptile was ever proffered. Similarly, the "yucca date worm" prominent in Laird's tales was never mentioned to me by the Kawaiisu, even though they knew and used the yucca plant.

In a social sense the Chemehuevi myths often have a warlike atmosphere; there are "armies" and "military leaders." Conflicts among the Kawaiisu were usually individual affairs. The group attack by the Bears upon Mountain Lion (Wolf) is an exception, but even here there is no clear sense of an organized movement.

According to Laird (1977a:100), "[Chemehuevi] mythic characters gamble incessantly. . . . Serious gambling is carried on night after night or day after day." Among the Kawaiisu, gambling is rarely mentioned, and it seems to have played a negligible role in the aboriginal culture. Setimo Girado alone tells a story in which gambling is a major motif.

However, myths at times embody customs which are not practiced by either tribe. Thus, in both the Chemehuevi and Kawaiisu tale called (in this collection) "Coyote Marries His Daughter," "Coyote, feigning approaching death, tells his wife and children to place his body on a funeral pyre, ignite it, and leave 'without looking back'--it being his intention to roll away from the flames unobserved, make off, and return with a new identity" (Laird 1977a:102; cf. the relevant myth here). Yet what Laird says of the Chemehuevi disposal of the dead is true also of the Kawaiisu: ". . . the Chemehuevi always buried their dead and burned the possessions of the deceased" (ibid.).

In the following illustrations of Kawaiisu and Chemehuevi correspondences, the Chemehuevi examples are taken, with one exception (#10), from Laird's book (1976).

(1) In the Chemehuevi "How People Were Made" (1976:149ff), Louse ($poo?^wavi$), nude except for a front apron which flaps up and down "to the rhythm of her motion, as she walked or ran . . . went along singing." Her "great beauty and the way she moved and the movements of her little apron and the song she sang all combined to drive Coyote mad with desire." Coyote tells her what he wants from her. Louse is agreeable but says he must build a house so that they may have privacy. He does so, but she wishes him into a deep sleep and she walks past the house without entering. He overtakes her three times, and the same thing happens. She escapes and eventually becomes the mother of mankind.

Coyote, in the Kawaiisu "Coyote and Louse" tale, sees a beautiful woman coming up the canyon. She is nude except for a breechclout and she jiggles her large breasts as she walks along singing. Coyote is mad with desire. He rushes ahead and builds a house which he makes look old. She passes it by. He does the same thing two more times and then pursues her, catches her, and tells her what he wants. He is about to copulate with her when she disappears. He finds her on his penis in the form of a louse (po?ovi). He is disgusted with the louse and throws it away.

(2) In the same Chemehuevi tale (pp. 151-2), Wolf and Coyote argue about how people should propagate themselves. Wolf suggests that "the embryo should form and grow in the little hollow at the back of a woman's wrist." Coyote says, "That is no good at all! That is too magical, too easy, it would not be any fun!" Then he sets forth his own ideas about the relationship between the sexes and the conception of children. To this day the old people say, "And we follow Coyote."

In "The Origin of Copulation," the Kawaiisu Coyote is portrayed as experimenting with sex. At first he thinks that women should have their vaginas on the edge of their right hands between thumb and forefinger. He tries copulation there, but it is so "strong" that he ejaculates as he approaches. "No," he says, "that's too strong. I want it to last longer." Then he puts it where it belongs. He got it just where he wanted it. "That's perfect," he said. So he left it there. (There are other Kawaiisu versions of this theme, but they give about the same information.)[7]

(3) In the Chemehuevi "How Cottontail Conquered the Sun" (pp. 152ff), Cottontail comes upon two small children sound asleep. Curious as to what is inside their little potbellies, he makes a tiny hole in one of them and finds that the child has eaten some small seeds (apparently *aka*, tansy-mustard) and some yucca dates, and has drunk a little water.

In the Kawaiisu "Cottontail and the Sun," Cottontail meets several sets of children. The grandmother of the Antelope children feeds *aka* (tansy-mustard seeds) to him and the children. Cottontail mixes the seeds with water and drinks the concoction. So do the children. Together they play "see-saw" on a log. Cottontail moves the log so rapidly and shakes it so hard that the children fall down and break open. The *aka* spills out of them.

(4) The central motif of the Chemehuevi "How Wildcat Brothers Recovered Their Hunting Song" (pp. 154ff) is not to be found among the collected Kawaiisu tales, but other incidents are clearly cognate. The oldest Wildcat brother wounds a jackrabbit, but the arrow remains stuck in the animal's body. When Wildcat finally overtakes and kills him, Wildcat finds himself on top of the sky. He comes to a house in which a man ("grandfather") is preparing to gamble with the rabbits who come every night to play. In the course of the game, the "grandfather," who is really Sun Spider, casts his net (web) around the area. The rabbits lose everything and, when they try to leave, they are caught in the net and killed. Sun Spider lets Wildcat down to earth through the sky-hole on a thread.

In the Kawaiisu "Wildcat and 'Man'," Wildcat pursues the jack-rabbit through a hole in the sky. The arrow drops down at the edge of the sky-hole. Wildcat walks along and kills a cottontail. He comes to a man's

---

[7]Thompson (1929:288): "The correcting of the location of the sexual organs or the method of giving birth appears in myths throughout the western half of the continent."

15

house and cooks the cottontail at the fire inside. He gives some of the roasted meat to the man. At night the rabbits come to gamble. While the rabbits are inside, Wildcat and the man set up a net around the house. Toward daylight the rabbits start for home, but they get tangled in the net and are killed. This happens every night. Finally the man takes the net, makes it into a cord, and lets Wildcat down to earth through the sky-hole.

(5) The Chemehuevi "How the Pleiades Came to Be" (pp. 156-7) is centered about the illness of one of Coyote's daughters. A shaman is summoned. Sending Coyote away on a trumped-up errand, the shaman reveals to the family that the girl is pregnant with Coyote's child. The afterbirth[8] is expelled and Coyote's wife thrusts it into the hot ashes of the campfire. Then, together with the shaman, the family goes up to the sky. Coyote returns, smells the meat roasting, and eats it. He looks up, sees the family and the shaman among the stars, and says, "You will become the Pleiades."[9] His wife responds, "You will . . . become a scavenger!"

These plot elements are to be found in two separate Kawaiisu tales. In "Coyote and His Pregnant Daughter," Coyote sends for the curing shaman, Hummingbird, because his daughter is ill. Hummingbird doctors her and discovers that she is pregnant. He accuses Coyote of impregnating her, but Coyote denies it. Coyote sends for another doctor, Mallard, and gets the same diagnosis.

The second episode of the Chemehuevi myth constitutes the conclusion of some versions of the Kawaiisu "Coyote Marries His Daughter" tale, as well as of the "Coyote and the Canada Geese" story. In every instance parturition follows the day of conception.[10] Coyote's family or the Canada Geese Girls flee to the sky where, in either case, they form the Pleiades, while Coyote, failing to reach them or to persuade them to come back, dies.

(6) In the Chemehuevi "How the Length of the Seasons Was Determined" (pp. 157f), Coyote and Burrowing Owl have an argument about the proper length of the seasons. The latter insists that they should have three months each, but Coyote says four. Burrowing Owl goes outside and "began to utter his own peculiar cry: *parangkwingkwi?i.* "Coyote" rushed into the thicket to investigate the strange noise. Burrowing Owl assumed his alternate form of Rattlesnake and promptly bit him."

The Kawaiisu account of the discussion of the length of the seasons is embedded in several stories, but principally in "The Race from Victorville to Koso Hot Springs."[11] The debate is between Coyote and the Lizard

---

[8]Anatomically it would appear more logical that the fetus (or fetuses) rather than the afterbirth was roasted in the ashes. See the Kawaiisu versions.

[9]Laird (1976:92) derives the word for Pleiades from *soniyavɨ*, an 'animal nest'. Kawaiisu Pleiades is recorded as *caniyo?ovɨ* and 'animal nest' as *sonivɨ*. There may be an error in the recording of the initial Kawaiisu letter.

[10]Thompson (1929:309) provides a bibliography on the subject of "short pregnancy" but it is incomplete.

[11]The discussion about the length of the seasons is to be found in the myths of other Great Basin groups. Lowie (1924:222-3) records two. In both it is Coyote who argues for longer seasons--twenty months in one story and forty in another. Thompson (1924:288) lists additional sources.

Brothers. As in the Chemehuevi account, Coyote argues for longer--much longer--seasons. Fortunately, he is overruled. When the sun shines again, it is spring. Coyote goes out and, according to some versions, eats the berries of the boxthorn bush (*Lycium andersonii*). He puts them in his mouth and says, *paaraʔwe*. As soon as he does that, a rattlesnake bites him and he dies.

(7) In the Chemehuevi story "The Journeys of Southern Fox" (pp. 159f), wherever one of the arrows of Southern Fox pierces the earth, water springs forth. In a comparable Kawaiisu episode, when Wolf and Coyote are crossing the desert, the former obtains water by plunging his arrow into the ground.

(8) The Chemehuevi "How Yucca Date Worm Girls Went to Look for a Husband" (pp. 162-8)[12] contains a series of incidents, three of which are to be found in separate Kawaiisu stories.

Red Racer (a snake) pierces his body on a thornbush and, crying *paɨɨ guruguruguru*, catches his dripping blood in a buckskin bag. He takes the blood home as food. In the Kawaiisu tale "Coyote and Red Racer," the snake goes under a thornbush and, moving back and forth under the thorns, scrapes meat off his back as he says *hudukugurɨ*. He takes the meat home as food.

In the same Chemehuevi myth Bat, a poor hunter, brings home ice instead of meat. He calls it "ice-fat" and tells the Yucca Date Worm Girls to eat it "raw"; i.e., without roasting. Bat, in the Kawaiisu story "Coyote and Bat," ashamed of his inability to catch game, brings home icicles which he calls "ice-fat"; he says the melting ice is really fat. In one version he faces the wall as he eats so that people will not know the truth.

The Chemehuevi Yucca Date Worm Girls finally find an ideal husband in Red-Tailed Hawk, who instructs them to sleep outside a cave while he is away and under no circumstances to enter the cave. It starts to rain and so, despite the warning, they decide to sleep in the cave. Along comes an old man (Grasshopper) and there is a discussion about where he should sleep. He rejects the suggestions that he sleep by the side of the fire, or crosswise at the girls' feet, or between them, but he accepts the idea that he should sleep crosswise at their heads. In the morning the girls say, "What a nice old man! He never even stretched all night long!" Just then he kicks out across their faces, gouging out their eyes.

In one of several Kawaiisu "Giant" tales, the two Quail sisters are warned by Squirrel Hawk, husband of one of them, not to sleep in a certain sandy wash because it is the pathway of the Giant (a grasshopper). They sleep there anyway. The Giant comes along and wants to sleep there, too. They tell him to sleep on one side of them. He says, "No." In between them? "No." On the other side of them? "No." At their feet? "No." At their heads?" "Yes," he says, he will sleep there. The sisters ask him if he stretches. He says, "No." In the morning they say he was very good not to have stretched. Just then he stretches and puts out their eyes with his toes.

(9) The Chemehuevi "How Wolf and Coyote Went Away" (pp. 192-207) and the Kawaiisu "Wolf ("Mountain Lion")[13] and Coyote" run parallel in most of

[12]A similar but shortened story is recorded by Lowie (1924:177-9) under the title "The Traveling Women."

[13]In some Kawaiisu versions the pair are Wolf and Coyote, in others Mountain Lion and Coyote. To retain the parallelism with the Chemehuevi story, I here keep to the Wolf-Coyote combination.

their details, but there are differences. The Chemehuevi Coyote, following Wolf's instructions, kills Aunt Bear and brings her body and all her possessions home, but he leaves behind a "poker stick." When he goes back to get it, it jumps away calling, "I am going to tell!" In the Kawaiisu story, Bear falls into a trap made by Wolf and Coyote. Coyote is told to burn every part of Bear, but he neglects to dispose of one organ, apparently the spleen, which gets away and calls, "I'm going to tell on you!"

Duly informed, the Bear People, in the Chemehuevi myth, come as an army. Wolf puts special clothes on Coyote and keeps changing them, but the Bears unfailingly recognize Coyote. Then Wolf tells him to run straight north and not to look back. Coyote looks back and "an arrow pierced Wolf's heart. Immediately the Bears fell upon him and butchered him." In the Kawaiisu tale the Bears come, and Wolf disguises Coyote so that the Bears will mistake Coyote for himself. But the Bears recognize Coyote no matter what clothes he wears. At length Wolf makes himself small and invisible, and gets out of his house through an elderberry-wood flute. He warns Coyote not to look back, but Coyote looks back and Wolf is hit with many arrows and cut into pieces. The Chemehuevi Coyote goes "to see if he could find any pieces of his brother's body. He found one sliver of bone, one little hair, one speck of dried blood, and one flake of flesh. These he gathered up carefully and put under a large basket." In the Kawaiisu tale, Coyote looks for some piece of his brother and finds a small rock on which is a drop of blood. He puts it in a large basket (of water?) and waits. After a few days he finds Wolf alive but lacking eyes.

In both the Chemehuevi and Kawaiisu myths, Coyote goes to the Bears' camp to recover Wolf's missing parts. Information is obtained from an old woman (or women). The Chemehuevi Coyote participates (with his *alter ego*, his penis)[14] in the Bears' Scalp Dance and recovers Wolf's scalp. The Kawaiisu Coyote participates in the Bear's Dance of the Eyes and gains possession of Wolf's eyes. There is a chase, and both Coyotes finally get home by riding in the seedpod of a bladderweed (in one Kawaiisu version, he rides in an acorn cupule). The endings of the stories differ, however. The Chemehuevi Wolf runs northward and, though Coyote tries to overtake him, he apparently never does. The Kawaiisu brothers decide to go to the end of the world, and they are there even now in the form of rocks. When they move, they cause earthquakes.

(10) Another Chemehuevi myth with obvious Kawaiisu correspondence is outlined by Laird in a brief paper (1974:220-4). It is concerned with Coyote's mother-in-law who lives with him and his family. Coyote invites her to go with him on an overnight jackrabbit hunt. When they lay down for the night, he rapes her with his sky-penis and she dies.[15] Coyote asks his tail how he should explain this to his family and is advised to say that they had been attacked, that his mother-in-law had been killed, and he had been severely wounded. To substantiate this, he pokes a hole in his belly and stuffs

---

[14]Though Coyote's penis as an *alter ego* was not recorded for the Kawaiisu, his tail on occasion serves a somewhat similar purpose. Laird (1974:223, fn. 11) refers to Coyote's tail, and adds, "Or penis. Coyote's alter ego may be referred to in either way."

[15]Laird (1977b:50-51) refers to this incident in a recent paper: Coyote "apparently has or retains from the beginning a mysterious sky-penis . . . with which he rapes and kills his mother-in-law."

jackrabbit intestines in, letting some of them hang out. From this point the tale has the "Coyote Marries His Daughter" motif of the supposed burning of Coyote's body on a pyre. His son not only sees him rolling off but also recognizes his father "by the peculiar way in which his teeth had been scored by a firestick." (In the Kawaiisu story the son sees his father rolling off and later observes that one of Coyote's teeth has four holes drilled into it.)

In the Kawaiisu myth, the mother-in-law episode is at times a prologue to the "Coyote Marries His Daughter" tale. He sleeps apart from his mother-in-law in a cave and makes a scratching noise on the wall. This frightens her. He repeats this action and the third time she jumps into his bed. They copulate all night, and in the morning she is pregnant. He shoots and kills her, and tells his family that she has been killed by "enemies."

THE COYOTE "CYCLE"

Most of the sixty-five Kawaiisu stories presented here have Coyote as a central character, but his conflicting roles make him a complex and enigmatic personality.[16] It is tempting to theorize that his several types of behavior originated in separate individuals who somehow, in the course of time, were combined into one. But such a supposition is untenable, at least within a single culture, since Coyote's amazing diversity is characteristic of him in many traditions and may, in a sense, be considered "normal." Since it is impossible to trace his development over the centuries, we must accept him as we find him in the myths.

In episodes involving the animal-people as a whole, he is usually the "chief" or the "idea man," but never the hero. In the creation story entitled "Earth Diver," it is Coyote who understands that there is soil beneath the water and that it must be brought to the surface to form dry land; but like all of the animals except Coot, the water fowl, he fails to bring it up. However, when the others despair that Coot will never reappear after his dive, Coyote assures them that he will. Apparently it is Coyote who places the tiny bit of soil on a winnowing tray and mixes it with peppergrass seeds which swell tremendously (when cooked). The people subsist on dirt until Coyote warns that this habit, if continued, will dissipate the earth on which they must dwell. Instead, he introduces the consumption of flora and fauna. He opposes death at first, but comes to accept it as a means of preventing overcrowding. He fixes the proper location of the sex organs and sets the ideal duration for the act of copulation. Little wonder, then, that after the animal-people exclude him from the winterhouse—where they are waiting for the return of the Sun—Coyote persuades them to relent by using a most convincing argument: "Without me, who will think for you?"

On the other hand, "Coyote always spoils things." Thus when the Sun is extinguished, it is discovered that as Mallard quacks and Owl hoots the light begins to return. But Coyote also insists on participating, and

---

[16]It should be noted that several myths involve Coyote even though he is not mentioned in the titles—such are "A Division of Labor," "The *Miitiipi*," "Owl's Wife," "The Origin of Copulation," and others, as well as some versions of other stories.

his singing/hollering plunges the world into darkness again. And when at last Sun is shining, Coyote goes forth and (according to some versions) urinates on an edible plant. Indeed, urination is a favorite trick of his. He thus befouls the spring used by himself and his brother, forcing the latter to find another water source. In "The Race from Victorville to Koso Hot Springs," he urinates on all the animals as he passes them. He argues with the Lizard Brothers about the proper length of the seasons--he offers no reason for wanting long winters--but fortunately he is overruled.

Among Coyote's most obvious traits are his insatiable sexuality and his irrepressible imitativeness. In his sex drive, he is bound by no physical limitations or moral considerations. Whether the situation calls for copulation with one female or five poses no problem for him. Impregnation always occurs immediately and offspring are born the next day. As my old female informant remarked, "What a man!" His propensity for imitation is based on the principle "If you can do it, I can do it," and he disregards all warnings to the contrary. As a result, he always fails and he always dies. Sometimes he seeks to duplicate the wondrous feats of Fox, Goldfinch, Hummingbird, and others, and sometimes as host he tries to obtain food for a guest in the same manner as the guest did for him when their roles were reversed. But the consequence is the same--he fails and dies. There are also a few puzzling incidents in which Coyote somehow resents hearing his name called--or even sounds that seem to mimic it. His attempt to silence such "name calling" brings him, as usual, to grief. Many of the stories of Coyote's exploits are the common property of neighboring peoples, and it is futile to look for a local motivation. However, the incident in which Coyote as host promises a "star-shirt" to his prospective guests even though no such garment exists appears, in my reading, to be without parallel.[17]

Among his various talents Coyote has the ability to make new things look old. Thus he deceives his family when they come to stay with his "friend" (himself) who lives on the other side of the mountain. He arrives ahead of them and manages to build an old house and spring and to scatter skins and old bones around as though he had lived there a long time. He uses the same technique when he seeks to seduce Louse.

Coyote has no patience. He finds it difficult to await the outcome of an action which he has initiated. In "Coyote and Mountain Lion," the two brothers set a trap for Bear. To restrain himself until morning to learn whether the plan is successful gives Coyote a restless night. Later, when his brother is "killed" by the Bears and Coyote finds a drop of his blood on a stone, the plan of restoring Mountain Lion's life by keeping the stone with the drop of blood in a basket (apparently covered with water) is almost too much for Coyote. He gets little sleep. In another context, when his "adopted" sons tell him they have killed a deer, he is hard put to wait until dawn so that he may go after the animal.

Since he seduces his daughter and mother-in-law, he cannot be

---

[17]On one occasion Sadie Williams told Cappannari that the "star shirt" was so called because it was brilliantly white. However, she gave no indication that such a shirt ever existed.

considered as having high moral principles. Yet he would like to hide his profligacy whenever possible. Discovering that he has made his mother-in-law pregnant, he kills her and invents a story that renders him blameless. When he learns that his daughter is "ill," he calls a curing shaman; but when the shaman informs him that he (Coyote) has impregnated her, he angrily dismisses the doctor and hires another. However, the diagnosis remains the same.

Despite the occasional admission that he is "smart" or "wise," Coyote is never represented as popular with his contemporaries. On the contrary, his repeated downfall is greeted with satisfaction. Even his wife exhibits no sorrow at his death (he was never a good provider). His protagonists are apt to remark, "Thus I kill you. You are already nothing!"

MISCELLANEOUS OBSERVATIONS

The mythological age is the day of the animal-people, but the relationship between that era and modern times is neither clear nor consistent. While it is generally conceded that the animal-people eventually become animals in habits and appearance, it is also apparent that certain typical animal traits are present from the beginning. Bat has poor eyesight; but when placed in the proper position in relation to his quarry, he is an excellent hunter. As he enters a house at night, his fluttering wings cause the flame to go out; later he is found clinging to the wall. Turtle can't jump and thus is no match for Coyote in a jumping contest. Rattlesnake is unable to proceed quickly because she has no legs. In an emergency, Coyote carries her around his neck, but she annoys and frightens him by causing her tongue to dart out. Skunk is not only mean, as admitted by his mother, but when angered "breaks wind like a fog." Even at a distance, the smell causes Snowbird to "die." The "old woman" who looks after Mountain Lion's sons is a gopher, but this is not observable until she is subjected to Mountain Lion's anger when she fails to prevent Coyote from kidnapping the boys; then she scurries into a gopher hole. At this point in the telling of the story, either Marie Girado or her daughter Clara commented, "That's the way those people were--like people until they were frightened and then they turned into animals."

There are other instances of transformation. Fortunately Coot had both fingernails and toenails in early times so that he was able to bring soil from under the water to form the earth's surface. In her brief account of the "Bears at Walker Basin," Martina Collins notes that after the bears were tired of dancing and tossing the stone ball around "they turned into real bears. They lost their hands and went up into the mountains." Louse is a beautiful woman and Coyote is overcome by her physical charm, but when he is about to copulate with her she becomes a louse on his penis; he throws it away in disgust. Dog was apparently able to talk like other animal-people, but because he spoke disparagingly of people when he saw them engaged in sexual intercourse, he was forever silenced. In the "Coyote, Hummingbird, and Rattlesnake" tale, Hummingbird is in the process of removing all of Rattlesnake's teeth. Were it not for Coyote's interference, he might have been successful. As it is, rattlesnakes still have four teeth.

Since the animal-people have the same appetites as humans, it is to be expected that they go after game: deer, rabbits, squirrels, rats. Therefore, obviously there are the hunters and the hunted, but both are essentially animals. Depending upon the plot situation, the roles may be interchanged. Thus Cottontail is the leading character in the "Cottontail and the Sun" myth but a victim in "Wildcat and Man." Deer, the favorite meat food of the Kawaiisu, has an ambivalent place in mythology. The origin of deer hunting involves a boy who is persuaded to act like a deer. At first deer meat is deemed too dry and lean, but this condition is rectified with the addition of human fat. The Kawaiisu prove themselves so superior as deer hunters that other peoples come to them for deer meat. In "Rat and Deer" (or "The Hoodwinked Dancers"), two animals who are usually among the hunted confront each other with deadly consequence. Rat uses the sharp-pointed yucca leaves as his weapon while Deer employs his horns. When Rat dies, "they discovered that he was a rat." In mythological times, Bluejay had long hair which she tied behind her head with tule. Later, her hair became her tail.

Occasionally a narrator will preface his story with the explanation that the tale he is about to tell is "true" and is concerned with "real people." Before the story has ended, however, the "man" or "woman" is likely to turn out to be one of the animal-people. Thus the "old man" in the "Wildcat and Man" tale is actually a "robin-like bird" whose Kawaiisu name is *kokopazi*. The "old lady" who is a weather shaman is a small bird, *puuciigiigi?ibɨ*, probably a titmouse or a pinyon bird. Some versions of "A Visit to the Underworld" refer to "old men" who (according to Setimo Girado) are deer, but more often the central character is Yahwera, who seems to have an affinity with mountain quail. The situation is more complicated in "Eagles Rescue a Man" since the man is represented as a human who climbed to a high point in the mountains and could not get down without the assistance of young eagles. He is greeted by friends who despaired of his returning.[18] "A Gambling Story" relates the adventures of the devil (*ɨnɨpɨ*) and his daughter; as previously suggested, it does not appear to be a Kawaiisu story. Again, "The Story of *Pogwitɨ*" does not seem to come within the category of mythology. Perhaps the same should be said of "The Story of Cannibalism."

Not infrequently myths are vehicles for explanations of natural phenomena. The reasons for the existence of some rock formations and certain characteristics of animals and plants are incorporated in the folktales. Thus I have seen the bare, narrow slide caused by Chipmunk as he slid down into Jawbone Canyon to get a better shot at game. A range of hills with saddles in between is accounted for by the flight of Falcon as he raced Coot; Falcon struck the range along the way and thus created saddles between peaks. A protruding rock surrounded by shattered pieces is all that is left of the projected bridge from Nichols Peak (the footprint of the great bird who broke down the bridge was said to have been visible until recently, when it was deliberately chipped off and taken away). Other noteworthy places remain a mystery: the winding trail which Rattlesnake made on his way to the river, the rocky trail which Mountain Lion used to get to his spring, the standing

---

[18]Thompson (1930:316) provides a bibliography relating to "helpful animals."

rocks which were formerly people in Kelso Canyon, and those other rocks which were once Doodle Bug, the arsonist, and Cottontail who killed him with a stone. And somewhere there is the flat rock on which Coyote lay when snow covered him (it is said to mark his body, including his scrotum). One consultant said that Coyote's rock-house with its ventilation holes is in the mountains.

As noted above, the origin of some of the distinctive features of animals is indicated by myths. The streaks on the face of the mountain lion and the spot on the neck of the cottontail are accounted for by the "Coyote Kidnaps Mountain Lion's Sons" story. The crest on the head of a titmouse (or whatever bird the weather shaman is) stems from the weather-making device she kept on the top of her head. The bill of the hummingbird comes from Coyote in the form of awls in payment for medical services to Coyote's pregnant daughter. Coyote gave pitch to Mallard in payment for similar services, and the pitch may be seen today as a spot on the nose of mallards. The rattlesnake's dental situation, as already pointed out, is attributed to the skill of Hummingbird, who attempted to extract all his teeth. Bluejay's long tail, as noted, is a transformation of her hair. Incidentally, if her mother-in-law had not interfered, mankind (i.e., Indians) might have been able to subsist on a few acorns instead of requiring many.

Plant lore was also influenced by mythology. The tips of yucca leaves are brown because they were stained with the blood of Deer when Rat used the sharp points as weapons. Evening Snow (*Linanthus dichotomous*) opens its flowers only after sundown because the plants used to be people who were too lazy to get up in the morning. Unfortunately no myth explains why Coyote's dog is a plant—silky California broom (*Lotus procumbens*).

It is altogether possible that Kawaiisu lore included many more explanations of phenomena, but they were somehow never brought forth, either through inquiry or in the course of story-telling. As it was, many such data came to light quite unexpectedly. Often consultants could not understand the anthropologist's interest in such bits of incidental information. How much more might have been forthcoming as a result of persistent and repeated questioning!

The myths recognize that people speak a variety of languages. The Lizard Brothers converse with one another in a speech not understood by others. In "First Food and the Population Problem" Potato Bug (or whatever bug he is) speaks in a tongue identified as *pitadɨ* (i.e., Southern Californian). The inability to understand what the weather-shaman bird is saying creates a crisis which is resolved only when it is remembered that Rattlesnake knows the language—and thus is bi-lingual.

Songs included in the myths are relatively numerous, and there may well have been more if we had asked for them and had had means of recording them. Usually they do not lend themselves to translation, and often the narrators said either that they did not know the meaning or that there was no meaning. Some songs appear to have their source in an alien speech (e.g., those which have words containing the letter *l*) and this may be evidence that the story itself has been borrowed. Even in those instances where Kawaiisu words seem to be involved, there are often elements which are outside the

23

known grammatical categories. Perhaps these represent poetic or obsolete word-forms.

The variability and diversity typical of recorded Kawaiisu mythology make it impossible to discern a single well-established standard of behavior and ethics. The complexity of Coyote's personality illustrates the situation. He can weep copious tears over the death of his "friend" (who doesn't exist), but he has no hesitancy in killing his mother-in-law to avoid taking the blame for her pregnancy. Mountain Lion's weeping for his kidnapped sons and his search for them over the years would seem to illustrate a concern for children. Bat's killing of his brother and all members of his brother's family except an infant may support this idea. But in this tale the concern of the mother-in-law is for the arrow when her son-in-law is shot and rolls over. She says, "Don't break your brother's arrow!" A great deal of the killing and destruction seems to be for no other purpose than a desire to exhibit prowess (e.g., "Cottontail and the Sun" and "The Story of *Pogwiti*-- whether or not the latter tale is "true"). Mountain Lion does not take revenge on Coyote alone. He kills the members of Coyote's family.

The "lessons" of the myths, if any, remain obscure. Possibly there has been a gradual loss of some basic implications in the telling and retelling. In any case, neither the narrators nor the Kawaiisu listeners made comments to indicate that some ethical or moral point had been made. The comments were usually concerned with the *facts* of the story, rarely with any subtler meaning. Thus after Marie Girado had told the tale "The *Miitiipi*," she remarked, "That meant there was going to be colored people"; accordingly, Cappannari called the tale "The Origin of Negroes." But the allusion is far-fetched. As indicated in a footnote to the tale, a *miitiipi* is any animal or human who brings bad luck. In this case the *miitiipi* is a *black* lizard, and it is only for this reason that the idea of a Negro is introduced. Again, the interest aroused by the "Giant" stories is not on an abstract moral plane; it lies in the physical proof that such beings actually exist. Emma Williams' remark after recounting the bloody adventures of *Pogwiti* comes closer to an ethical judgment: "Everybody treated *Pogwiti* right. He killed lots of people, but when he came into anyone's house, they treated him right."

Recalling the absorption of both narrator and listeners as a myth was being recited, I sensed that what was involved was something more than entertainment, but far less than preachment. These modern descendants of an ancient people were catching a glimpse of that wondrous world where almost anything could happen. Freed for the hour from the problems and responsibilities of modern living, they envisioned the adventures of the animal-people who, though gone forever, had really existed in bygone days.

I would like to thank Tom Blackburn for encouraging me to bring the myths into publishable form, and for editing the manuscript and seeing it through the publishing process. I would also like to thank Larry Eckhart for drawing the map.

Kawaiisu Myths

1. Earth Diver[1]

A.   McCOWN (RAFAEL GIRADO)

In old times there was water all over the world. There was no land at all. The animals and birds were living up in the sky. Coyote sent them down one by one to bring dirt up from the bottom of the ocean. All of them tried but could not get any dirt. It was too far down. Coyote tried but he got only half-way down. He nearly drowned and had to come back up.

Finally a little black bird *potok*,[2] who lived in the water, dove down. He stayed down all day, and the other animals thought he was dead. Coyote said, "No, he isn't dead." At length the little bird came up. Coyote asked him, "Did you get any dirt?" He said, "Only a little." He scraped the dirt out from underneath his fingernails and toenails, and put it on a flat coiled tray. It made only a very little pile. The animals left it there and it grew bigger every day. Coyote said, "Good! Pretty soon we'll have a world." It kept getting bigger and soon covered all the water. It took a year for the dirt to grow into the earth. Then the animals came down out of the sky and lived on the land.

There were no trees or plants. The planter is Bluejay, but no one knew where he got the plants to start things growing. He still plants pinyon and acorn trees.

B.[3]   CAPPANNARI (MARIE GIRADO: CLARA GIRADO)

Long ago the animal-people knew a flood was coming. It was raining

---

[1]The story of the earth being formed when dirt was brought up from underneath the water is widespread in America. According to Thompson (1929: 279), muskrat is usually the one who dives and brings up soil. However, water birds also participate. Among the Western Mono, Duck, Coot, and Grebe dive. It is Grebe who is successful (Gifford 1923:304).

[2]Elsewhere McCown identifies *potok* as coot, though my later informants did not recognize the word. Kawaiisu words usually terminate in vowels.

[3]A similar myth is recorded for the neighboring Yauelmani Yokuts (Kroeber 1907:229). Duck dives down and comes up with a little dirt under its

very hard. They went up South Fork [of the Kern River] to the highest peak.
A few were drowned but many reached the peak. The rest of the world was
covered with water. The only land they could see was around their peak. They
grew tired of the flood.

Everyone dove into the water to try to bring up some dirt. Finally
they sent the bird *potok*[4] under the water and it came up with some dirt under
its nails. They put the dirt on a winnowing tray. Then they added a wild
plant (*soid*)[5] which swells tremendously when it is cooked. They mixed the
soid with the dirt, and the dirt began growing. They put the winnower on
the water. Now all the earth is sitting on a winnower.

The world was flat. Squirrel went along and turned up the hills
and burrowed the canyons. Bluejay planted the trees. They still plant trees
by dropping acorns, pinyons, and pine-nuts.

----

fingernail. Eagle mixed it with some ground seeds and water. It swelled
and spread everywhere. Cappannari called this tale "Flood Myth," but the
most important element is the establishment of dry land.

[4]Cappannari's informant could not identify *potok*. See McCown's
version.

[5]The plant is probably peppergrass, *Lepidium lasiocarpum*
(*sooiidɨbɨ*).

2. First Food and the Population Problem

A. McCOWN (RAFAEL GIRADO)

Coyote said, "There will be a lot of people." A little Bug (he lives in the ground) said, "There must not be too many people. They've got to die some time."

B. CAPPANNARI (MARIE GIRADO: CLARA GIRADO)

A long time ago there were millions of people. Above Bena[1] they sampled the earth. They ate up a whole mountain. Coyote said, "No, we must not eat dirt or there won't be any earth left.[2] It won't work." The people liked that earth, but they didn't eat any more. There is still a big hole there where they sampled the earth.

C. CAPPANNARI

Coyote said, "There will be a lot of people." No one had died yet. Potato Bug said people should live always. Coyote disagreed. He said, "No, the world will be too crowded." That is why people don't live forever.[3]

---

[1]Bena is a small station on the railroad route from the San Joaquin Valley up to Tehachapi Pass. The Kawaiisu use this name, but they also call the site *po?omo?osɨk^{w}eepiyaaka*, which refers to the nearby Kern River (see another version of this tale). Near this site the Indians used to gather an edible seed known as *maasita*. I was unable to obtain a specimen.

[2]That is, if people ate the dirt, there would be no place for them to live.

[3]The debate between Coyote and Bug as to whether people should live forever is a common theme. See, for example, Southern Ute (Lowie 1924: 2).

On this side of Bakersfield along the Kern River road there was a place called *po?omo?osɨkʷeepiyaaka*[5] where there were so many people they were just like trees in a forest. There wasn't enough food for all of them. They said, "What are we going to eat?" They started eating dirt. They took their basket hats[6] and scooped up the dirt. That left a big hole in the ground which is still to be seen. Coyote said that if they kept on eating dirt there would be no place left where people could live.

People didn't die. When they grew old, they would go and bathe, comb their hair, and become young again. Coyote and Bug[7] didn't like the way people became young again. Bug said that if they kept being young and having children, there would be too many people in the world. Coyote agreed. Bug said that whenever a person died there was one less. Coyote said that if he found a dead person he would eat him.

That is why people die.

There were lots of different people all around. Bug and Coyote were people, too. There wasn't enough food for all of them. Coyote said to Bug, "*Pikagoyu*,[8] what are we going to eat?" People were eating dirt. Because they ate dirt, they made many holes in the ground.

People didn't die when they grew old. They went and took a bath and came back young. "People should die," said Coyote, "the earth isn't big enough for all of us." Coyote said, "If anybody dies, I'll eat them." Bug, who talked the *pitadɨ* language,[9] said, "*amocok tɨɨvahac*," which was translated 'not enough room—dirt'. Bug eats dirt.

----

[4]Emma Williams told this story twice within a two-week period. For this version the translator was her granddaughter Elsie, but Elsie had recently married and had returned for a brief visit. The version which follows was translated by Emma's daughter, Sadie.

[5]The word means 'water coming around (the bend)' and refers to the Kern River. The area is also called Bena (see other versions).

[6]The common gear of women is the small coiled basket-hat which could serve various purposes.

[7]The Bug is described as "a large potato-eating bug with striped abdomen." Emma called it *hayɨ?mɨkɨzi* and Setimo *imižigɨzi*. They are not necessarily referring to the same insect.

[8]Coyote addresses Bug as "baldhead." *pika-* means 'smooth'.

[9]*pitadɨ(mɨ)* refers to one or more tribes south of the Kawaiisu. I have usually assumed that the Kitanemuk tribe is the one specifically designated, but the name was sometimes applied to the "Serrano."

They lived at a place near Bena. Coyote said, "There will be many people." Bug said, "There will be too many of us." Coyote said, "What will we eat?" "We will eat dirt," said Bug. They started eating dirt at Bena and made holes which are still to be seen. "No," said Coyote, "if we keep on doing this, we shall eat up all the dirt. We should eat acorns, pinyons, chia, and deer."

---

[10]Setimo combined three subjects in one narration. This is the first. The second is concerned with "The Origin of Deer" (q.v.), and the third is a discussion of the animals as to their future activities (q.v.).

3. The First Death[1]

A.   McCOWN (RAFAEL GIRADO)

Coyote was the first person to die. His daughters beat him and thought he was dead. They stuck a knife into him but it went into his belt and he was not killed. His wife thought he was going to die so she pulled him into the *togoni*.[2] Coyote said, "Go over the hill to some relations but, when you go, you must not look back."[3]

He tried to rape his daughters, but they beat him up again. Then they stuffed his mouth with a powder (*nara*).[4] It choked him and they tickled him so that he could not breathe and he died. They buried him in the rocks and put a big pile of rocks on top of the place. There was no fiesta. Only his wife, the girls, and one boy were there.

B.   ZIGMOND (SETIMO GIRADO)

Coyote died in the canyon.

Many people came and said, "Who's going to think for us now?" Coyote was very smart.

Worms came from the ground and went under Coyote. People beat him with a stick. "Get up!" they said. He was very hard to arouse. "I went sound asleep," said Coyote. He got up.[5]

---

[1]In the myths, "death" is not always terminal death. In one way or another the victim may recover.

[2]This word is probably *tɨgahni* 'cave' (lit. 'rock house').

[3]At this point McCown adds "etc." which would indicate that the remainder of the narrative is related elsewhere (cf. "Coyote Marries His Daughter"). Altogether this is a confused account.

[4]This must be pounded *naara* seeds (melic grass, *Melica imperfecta*).

[5]"The act of reviving a dead person by beating him and the statement of the revived person that he was only sleeping occurs in both Western Mono and Northern Shoshone" (Gifford 1923:304).

4. The Origin of Copulation[1]

A.
ZIGMOND (SETIMO GIRADO)

Coyote caught a girl and had intercourse with her. He said it was too much (?)--it was no fun. He tried again and it was too short. He said, "I want it a little longer. Then it will be good. I'm going to try again." This time it took 10 to 15 minutes. "That's how I want it," said Coyote.

B.
CAPPANNARI (MARIE GIRADO: CLARA GIRADO)

Coyote decided that women should have their vaginas on the edge of their right hands, between the thumb and the forefinger. He tried it there, but it was so powerful that he would ejaculate as he approached it. "No," he said, "that's too strong. I want it so it will last longer." Then he put it back where it belongs. He got it just where he wanted it. "That's perfect," he said. So he left it there.

C.
CAPPANNARI (MARIE GIRADO: CLARA GIRADO)

When Coyote first tried it, it didn't last very long, and he didn't like it. He said, "There will have to be a better way." He tried it again. He said, "It should take a little longer. It will be better that way." He said, "This time it's better." So now everyone has it this way.

---

[1]"The correcting of the location of the sexual organs or the method of giving birth appears in myths throughout the western half of the continent" (Thompson 1929:288).

5. The Origin of Deer Hunting

A.
ZIGMOND (EMMA WILLIAMS: ELSIE GARCIA)

There were two girls and a boy. An old man wanted to turn the boy into a deer. The sisters wept because they didn't want this to happen to their brother. People said that unless this was done, there wouldn't be any deer. They said that when men would hunt deer, they might be bitten by a rattlesnake or killed by a grizzly bear, so that the deer wouldn't be the only one to die. Finally the boy gave in and consented.

They turned the boy into a deer. They put horns on his head. They dressed him in a deerskin and sewed it up the front. They glued hoofs on his feet with pitch. Then they made him stand up, and told him to go up on the hill to try it out. He went up on the hill and started to eat grass.[1]

People went up to hunt him. All the different tribes tried to kill him, but he would discover them and run away. The Kawaiisu man was the only one who didn't go after him. The others told him to try. When he started out, the others threw dirt at him and called him 'frog'.[2] They said he wouldn't get the deer. The wind was blowing. The other tribes were watching. The Kawaiisu man crawled toward the deer in the direction of the wind. He killed the deer. The others all clapped their hands.

The old man skinned the deer. All the tribes got a piece of the meat. They all built fires and cooked the meat. But it was dry; it had no fat. The old man said it would taste better if it had some fat on it. One of the old men cut fat from himself and wrapped it around the deer's heart. That is why there is fat around the heart.

People still have dreams of this place where the deer was first made. The other tribes said that henceforth this tribe would hunt deer and others would buy it from them. And that's how it was. The South Fork [Tübatulabal] and Bakersfield [Yokuts] people didn't kill deer. They got it from this tribe.

-----

[1]I did not record the Kawaiisu word here, but it was probably *mahavɨ* which refers to wild vegetation in general rather than grass specifically. See Setimo Girado's version.

[2]The connotation of 'frog' was not explained.

"You will be deer," Coyote said to that boy. The boy's mother wept because of his saying that. "All right," said the boy, "I will become deer." Coyote said, "Go over there and eat *mahavɨ*."[4] "All right," said Coyote, "shoot him." But they couldn't kill him. Whenever Bluejay saw a hunter, he cried out and the deer ran away scared. "Call Mountain Lion; let him hunt that one." Then Mountain Lion hunted deer and killed him. "All right," said Coyote, "now let's eat." Then they roasted it. It tasted bad; they got a stomach ache from it. When it was roasted, it burned because it had no fat. They ate it with the hide.

Two (men) greased the deer's flesh with fat. "All right," said Coyote, "let's roast it again. Now, let's eat it. There, now it's going to be good."

"It tastes good," said Coyote.

C.   CAPPANNARI[5]

The Indians first came from this side of Santa Maria. All the tribes lived there together.[6]

An old man [a "real" old man; i.e., not one of the characters, semi-animal, who lived in Coyote's time][7] said he wanted to make deer. His brothers didn't want to be deer. They[8] both cried. The man put horns and hoofs on them. He made the hoofs out of a paste. After he made those deer, they went up into the mountains. They were bucks.

---

[3]This episode is the second of three which Setimo put together in one narrative. See "First Food and the Population Problem" and "The Discussion of the Animals." It was the first time I had attempted to take the dictation in Kawaiisu.

[4]Though *mahavɨ* was often translated 'grass', it has a broader meaning. 'Unplanted vegetation' is a more accurate definition. In another myth it clearly refers to a tree. During our ethnobotanical sessions, Emma Williams would indicate that a plant was useless by calling it *mahavɨ*.

[5]Cappannari does not name his narrator here, but it was probably Emma Williams, with Sadie Williams as translator.

[6]At this point Cappannari has the following note: "The reference to a time when all the tribes lived in Santa Maria, which is west of Bakersfield and near the coast, is unusual for a Shoshonean-speaking people who so rarely have myths referring to migrations or past locations."

[7]While consultants not infrequently insist that certain individuals are "real" people in contradistinction to the usual animal-people, the difference is not to be taken too literally. In the other version given by Emma Williams, it will be noted that the "old man" takes fat from himself to improve the taste of the deer meat.

[8]Apparently the "old man" had two brothers.

Other tribes hunted them. They wanted to kill them but they
didn't succeed. Finally a Kawaiisu man did kill them. He dragged them down
the hill to his house. The deer had no fat. The old man put something
around their hearts to make them fat. Then they ate them.

D.   CAPPANNARI (MARIE GIRADO: CLARA GIRADO)

        This was in the beginning. Coyote and the others were deciding
what to eat. They picked out deer lady who had a son, a young boy. They
chose the boy to be killed as a deer. His mother didn't want her son killed,
and she cried. Coyote said, "Don't cry. He won't really die. His spirit
will rise." Before Coyote killed the deer boy, he said to him, "Right after
we kill you, you will get up. You will live even after we have made jerky
out of you."

        They ate some of the meat, but it wouldn't stay in their stomachs.
This was the first food people had ever eaten. They had stomach aches.
Coyote said, "Let's eat the meat with the fur[9] on it." They tried it that
way. Then it was good. They didn't get sick from it. After that, they
always ate deer meat.

_____

        [9]In light of the other versions of this myth, it is possible that
this word should be "fat."

6. The Discussion of the Animals[1]

A.   ZIGMOND (SETIMO GIRADO, PARTLY IN TEXT)

After deer was created and found to be good to eat, each animal declared what it would be and what would be its main source of food.

"I am going to be coyote," said Coyote. "I will eat dead things."
"What are you going to be?" he asked Eagle. "I am going to be an eagle," said Eagle. "I shall eat jackrabbits." "Good,"[2] said Coyote.
"What are you going to be?" Coyote asked Chicken Hawk. "I am going to be a chicken hawk," said Chicken Hawk. "I shall eat jackrabbits."
"And what are you going to be?" Coyote asked Falcon. "I am going to be a falcon," said Falcon. "I shall eat jackrabbits."
Squirrel Hawk said, "I shall eat jackrabbits."[3]
Bluejay said, "I shall eat pinyons."
Ground Squirrel said, "I shall eat pinyons and acorns."
Tree Squirrel said, "I shall eat the seeds of the digger pine (*Pinus sabiniana*)."
"And what will you be?" Coyote asked Rattlesnake. "I shall be very bad," said Rattlesnake. "My bite will cause (people) to die."
"I shall be good," said Gopher Snake.
"I shall be a grizzly bear," said Grizzly Bear. "I shall kill a person when I find him."
"I shall walk on the ground," said Stink Bug.
"I shall be watersnake," said Watersnake. "I shall eat gophers."
"I shall be dog," said Dog. "I shall eat good food."
"I shall be fox," said Fox. "I shall eat everything."
"I shall be wildcat," said Wildcat. "I shall eat Cottontail."
"I shall be skunk," said Skunk. "I shall eat Stink Bug."
Mountain Lion said, "I shall kill deer."

---

[1]A similar discussion is to be found in an account of the "Extinction of the Sun," but it is not as extensive as here.

[2]Kawaiisu *yo* is a connecting word which may be translated 'all right', 'good', etc.

[3]Squirrel Hawk was also identified as Rabbit Hawk. From this point I have omitted the framework of the dialogue though it ought to be assumed throughout.

Crow said, "I shall eat pinyons."
The *toko*,[4] the pinyon jay, the *puuciigiigi?ibɨ*[5]--all will eat pinyons.

Quail and Mountain Quail will eat grass seeds.
Dove said, "I shall eat *Mentzelia*[6] seeds."
Brown Bear said, "I shall be wild. I shall eat pinyons and acorns."

---

[4]The identity of the *toko* is not clear. Setimo said it is "a bird like a bluejay." Another consultant said it is "like a large mockingbird."

[5]Consultants variously called the *puuciigiigi?ibɨ* a 'pinyon jay', a 'pinyon bird', and a 'titmouse'.

[6]There are several species of edible *Mentzelia* seeds. The plants are popularly known as 'stickseed' and 'blazing star'.

7. How the Kawaiisu Got Fire

A. <u>McCOWN (SANTOS PHILLIPS SUPPLEMENTED BY RAFAEL GIRADO)</u>

There was neither fire nor pinyons around here. The people saw smoke but did not know what it was. The chief[1] sent Crow to see what it was. Crow flew to *kegutum*,[2] the highest mountain (above Randsburg in the desert). The only trees in the world were on *kegutum*. Bat (*patzazɨ*)[3] was the one who got the fire. When he came back with the fire, it was raining. He put the fire under his wings so as to keep it dry.

B. <u>McCOWN (EMMA WILLIAMS)</u>

Kotcakuz[4] was the one that did the stealing of fire from *kegutum*, and *atakuz*[5] helped him. *Keguta*[6] is the name of the mountain from which they stole the fire.

C. <u>McCOWN (CHARLEY HASLEM)</u>

Patzaz[7] was the one who stole the fire from *kouta*[8]--a place far distant in the east. The fire was in the inside of a white rock called *tocitumba*[9] and with this and *yesca*[10] from the inside of the white oak, the

---

[1]The chief is not named here, but elsewhere McCown notes that Coyote was the chief.

[2]The place is probably *keeguta*, the Panamint Range.

[3]A more accurate spelling is *paacaʔazi*.

[4]$K^{w}i\check{c}iʔaakazi$ is Yellowhammer.

[5]*Atakazi* is Crow.

[6]See note 2.

[7]See note 3.

[8]See note 2.

[9]*Tosotɨ(m)bi* 'white flint, pyrites'--used for strike-a-light. Fire might be conceived of as being *in* the rock.

[10]Spanish 'tinder, punk'; *yezkaʔa*--the spongy pith of dead trees used for starting fires.

fire was kindled.

D.   CAPPANNARI (MARIE GIRADO: CLARA GIRADO)

      A long time ago there was no fire around here. These people saw
smoke up at Panamint. Lots of them started up there to get that fire. When
they arrived, they asked the Koso[11] for the fire, but the Koso wouldn't give
them any. The Koso stayed awake all night because they didn't want the
Kawaiisu to get any fire. One Kawaiisu had a four o'clock flower.[12] He
blew it in the direction of the Koso and they all went to sleep. Bat took
the fire, put it under his wing, and started over here. All the Kawaiisu
followed him. Before they reached home, the Koso woke up and saw fire already here. They were angry and chased the Kawaiisu. They killed a lot of
those Kawaiisu.

---

    [11]The informant probably said *kohoži* who apparently lived in the
Panamint Range area. Cappannari and I identified them as 'Koso' or 'Panamint',
but perhaps 'Western Shoshoni' would be a suitable designation. The Kawaiisu
called themselves *niwi*, pl. *niwiwi*, 'people'. They never used the designation Kawaiisu.

    [12]Possibly a *Mirabilis* species, popularly known as 'four-o'clocks'.

8. How the Kawaiisu Got Pinyons

A.   <u>McCOWN (SANTOS PHILLIPS)</u>

    Acorns and chia were here already, but pinyons were lacking.
Tutupu[1] was the range of mountains on which the pinyons grew. *Pomtcaruv*,
Mouse,[2] smelled the pinyons tied in a sack on the top of a long pole.
Kitcakuz, Yellowhammer,[3] climbed the pole and got the pinyons. He knocked
the sack of pinyons off the pole with his tongue and *atakuz*, Crow,[4] got it.
Crow brought them back and gave them to the people. This all happened at
night. Two or three others tried to climb the pole and get the pinyons.
Pomtcaruv was one. People over there started fighting the people here. They
saw the fire and smoke of the people who were cooking pinyons here.

B.   <u>McCOWN (EMMA WILLIAMS)</u>

    Kotcakuz[5] was the one that brought the pinyons to the Kawaiisu,
but *atakuz* also brought some at the same time. He helped *kotcakuz*.

C.   <u>ZIGMOND (EMMA WILLIAMS)</u>

    On the other side of Lone Pine (to the north) was one pinyon tree
(*Pinus monophylla*) with many pinyon cones on it. The animals and birds were
gathered around the tree in circles. The animals and birds from here went
there to get some pinyons, but they couldn't get near the tree. One would
try to get over the rows of animals that guarded the tree, but he couldn't
get in between them because they were too close together. Then those from
here told Yellowhammer that, since he had long legs, he should step over the
rows. They tied thorns of the cottontop cactus (*Echinocactus polycephalus*)
to his legs to make them even longer. He stepped over one circle after

---

[1]The location of *tutupu* is unknown.

[2]In the Kawaiisu Dictionary, 'mouse' is *puˀmičagiži*.

[3]'Yellowhammer' is *kʷičiˀaakazi*.

[4]'Crow' is *atakazi*.

[5]See note 3.

another, seized a pinyon cone and got away without anyone around the tree knowing.

But when Yellowhammer got off a little distance they saw and pursued him. They all ran. He tired and they were about to overtake him, but he passed the pinyon cone to someone else. They hit Yellowhammer with a stick and killed him. As an animal tired, he passed the cone to another. At last Crow had it. He put it on his knee. The pursuers caught him and hit him with a stick. They looked all over him for the cone. His knee was swollen with "pus"--it was the pitch oozing out. They thought he was sick. They cut off his leg and threw it in this direction. That is why there are pinyons here. They killed Crow and went back.

When they were far away, they looked back and saw smoke coming from the place where they had killed Crow. They thought it was a mountain fire, but it was actually pinyons roasting. When they reached their tree, it was all dried up. There were neither leaves nor pinyons on it.

And there are no pinyons up there to this day.[6]

D.   CAPPANNARI[7]

Long ago there were no pinyon trees in the area around here. There was one pinyon tree on a mountain called *oworeze*.[8] It is above Bishop.

Lots of "people" went up there--birds, bears, etc. They wanted those pinyons. The people who owned the tree were lying in a circle around it. The ones who wanted the pinyons were behind them. Yellowhammer tied awls to his feet and crept through the ring of people. He licked the tree with his tongue and then crept back. The people got up and chased him. He ran until he was tired. Then he gave the pitch to Crow who put it on his knee and ran with it until he was too tired to go any further. The people caught him and thought the pitch (*sunup*)[9] on his knee was pus. They cut his knee and threw the pitch toward us [in Loraine].[10] Then they looked across the mountain and saw smoke there. They were already cooking pinyons here. The people were angry. They cried and then went back home.

---

[6]In a personal communication (1937) Gayton comments: "[This is the] 'Theft of Pinenuts' (Great) Basin tale; for general reference see Gayton (1935:590, fn. 50)."

[7]Although Cappannari omits the name of the narrator of this myth, it is likely that it was Emma Williams. There is a close parallel between it and the version given to me by Emma ten years earlier.

[8]No mountain of this name was identified. Conceivably this is Cappannari's transcription for Mount Whitney (*aragawiiya*), which is near Bishop.

[9]Pitch (or gum) is *sanapɨ*.

[10]Loraine was the site of a Kawaiisu community.

9. The Division of Labor[1]

A.

CAPPANNARI (MARIE GIRADO: CLARA GIRADO)

In the old times women used to do the hunting. Men didn't know how to hunt.

Bluejay lived up on Hopper Mountain where many animal-people lived. She wasn't married, and Coyote wanted her for his wife. He thought he could hunt as well as she could, so he took her arrow away from her. All the men went out hunting.

Coyote said that the best hunter would marry Bluejay. Red Bug [a small bug that eats its way into wood or skin and cannot be removed] went along. The others bet that Red Bug couldn't kill anything.

There was a long line of deer going over a mountain. Little Red Bug shot one arrow and it went through all of the deer, killing all of them. He proved to be the best hunter and was going to marry Bluejay.

Coyote was so angry and jealous he decided women wouldn't be hunters-- just men would be hunters. Bluejay was a good worker; she always pounded acorns.

Coyote always spoils everything.

_____

[1]As recorded by Voegelin (1938:53), the Tübatulabal have a more detailed "Division of Labor" myth. However, as with the Kawaiisu, the responsibility of hunting ultimately is assigned to the men.

10. The Bears at Walker Basin

A.

ZIGMOND (EMMA WILLIAMS: ELSIE GARCIA)

The bears had a fenced enclosure[1] in Walker Basin. They went through Havilah and Isabella to the river[2] and got a big round rock. As they came back, they tossed it to one another without dropping it. When they reached Walker Basin, they played ball with the rock. The little canyons running into the Basin are where they had to run to catch the rock. As they played, they sang a song: *hulaili pu.. hu yetipu hu..*[3]

One day Coyote and his brother Mountain Lion went there and ate with the bears. Coyote told them that they were going to make a fire and sleep outside, but the bears wanted him to play and dance with them. So he told his brother that he had been invited to play with them. Coyote dressed up and painted his face. He braided his hair and tied it around his head. He put eagledown on his head.[4] As he played with the bears, instead of singing with them he sang his own song: *yak^w ana yak^w ana mayɨni..kɨtana mayɨni.. kɨtana.*[5] He grew reckless and danced too near the fire. His tail caught fire,[6] but he kept on dancing. The bears told him his tail was burning, but he said it didn't matter. They were all frightened and ran away. Coyote was left alone and kept dancing, but since there was no one to dance with, he had to stop and put out the fire.

The Canada Geese, who had been at the celebration, left for Bakersfield--except one. That one was always to be seen at Walker Basin.[7] The

---

[1]The enclosure was probably formed with a circle of brush such as the Kawaiisu used for their celebrations.

[2]These towns are in an almost direct line north of Walker Basin. Isabella was on the Kern River--but is now covered by the man-made Lake Isabella.

[3]The word *yetipu* means Walker Basin.

[4]This description gives some idea of the personal preparation for a celebration.

[5]The meaning of the song is not clear.

[6]Coyote's "sparking" tail is mentioned in other myths.

[7]Emma Williams commented: "Maybe a white man killed it."

geese sang a song as they left: *ayarawičikahni po..či kahni po..či*[8] [repeated]. Coyote liked the song. He wanted to fly and sing like the geese. He flapped his hands and tried to fly, but he fell down. He sang the wrong song.

After a while, the bears grew tired of playing. They dropped the rock. A pool of water formed where they dropped it. Long ago the rock could be seen through the water.

B.   ZIGMOND (SETIMO GIRADO)

The two brothers, Coyote and Wolf, went to dance with the bears at Walker Basin. They had a picnic down there and a big dance. Everyone danced, and they danced all night. Coyote's tail was "sparking like a battery" at the top. His brother said, "What's the matter with you?" Coyote said nothing and kept on dancing.

An old lady[9] was packing wood all night for the fire. She lost her tobacco.[10] She said, "*puzinikaax*."[11] No one could understand her. Coyote said, "What did you say?" She repeated it. No one understood her. Coyote said, "I'm going to get Rattlesnake. She will know what she's saying." Coyote went after Rattlesnake. Coyote said, "I'm coming after you." "All right," said Rattlesnake. Coyote packed her--she had no legs. While he was packing her, her tongue kept shooting out. Coyote was afraid of it. Rattlesnake said, "I won't do anything." She said, "*haawigi*," but Coyote didn't understand her.

They went down to Walker Basin where there were many people. Rattlesnake asked the old lady, "What do you do?" They talked to one another in their own language. Rattlesnake understood what *puzinikaax* meant. It meant 'tobacco'. The old lady had said that she had lost her tobacco. They all looked for it and found it. They gave it to her.[12]

Coyote said to the bears, "We're going to play games this morning." They said, "All right." They used a large round stone as a ball. The bears and Coyote tossed it to each other. They batted it all around Walker Basin. That's why the Basin is flat. They all went after the ball and tossed it

---

[8]No meaning was suggested; *kahni* as a separate word means 'house'.

[9]The "old lady" is pinyon bird, *puuciigiigiʔibɨ*. No reason is given for her speaking a "foreign" language. Her name seems to be built on the stem *puucii-* 'star'. Could this be the basis for her being a weather shaman?

[10]In this version Pinyon Bird loses her tobacco. Elsewhere it is her knife.

[11]This transcription is only approximate. Ordinarily 'x' is not used for a Kawaiisu phoneme. Compare Cappannari's recording of the word. Some of the informants thought the language is Tübatulabal.

[12]The importance of finding the lost object is not mentioned in this version. If it had not been found, a heavy snow would have come.

again. Coyote tried to hit it first, but missed. The bears hit it good
all around the Basin. Coyote said, "I want to hit it, too." He ran after
it fast. Chicken Hawk got to it first and won the game.[13]

Coyote was angry. "I'm going to throw the ball into the water,"
he said. "I'm not going to play with this ball anymore." He put it in the
water. Long ago people could still see it floating around.

Coyote carried Rattlesnake back to where she lived. "I'm going to
live here forever," she said. There are still many rattlesnakes there. It
is called *togowagahnivɨ*, 'Rattlesnake's House'.[14]

C.   CAPPANNARI (EMMA WILLIAMS: SADIE WILLIAMS)

The bears had a feast in Walker Basin. Pinyon Bird went to get
firewood for them. She had a string tied around her head and she carried her
knife there. While she was gathering wood, she lost her knife.[15] She came
back and said to the bears, "*puzine kut kut kut*."[16] The bears couldn't understand her. They asked Coyote what she said, but he couldn't understand her
either. The bears told Coyote to go over to *ayapiiya*[17] and get Snake who
understood Pinyon Bird's language. They talked together all the time.

Coyote ran over to Snake's house. Snake was sitting in a basket
which she was making. Coyote told Snake they needed her because no one could
understand Pinyon Bird's language. Snake put away her basket. She said to
Coyote, "I can't walk very fast." Coyote said, "I'll carry you." Snake's
head was over Coyote's shoulder and her tongue was out. Coyote saw it and
was frightened. He dropped her. Snake asked, "Why did you drop me?" Coyote
said he was afraid. He picked her up, and the same thing happened several
times. Snake said, "I won't bite you. I just do that [i.e., hold out my
tongue]."

Finally they got there. Snake talked to Pinyon Bird and then told
the bears that she had lost her knife. "It's going to snow if you don't find
her knife." That bird was a rainmaker. The women took their little baskets
and looked for the knife. They sifted dirt through the baskets and found the
knife.

---

[13]The procedure of the game is not clear.

[14]This is the placename given to a canyon north of Walker Basin.

[15]The word given (*siavarena*) is not the usual Kawaiisu word for
knife. One informant thought it comes from Tübatulabal.

[16]No translation was given for these words. They should be compared with those recorded in the Zigmond version.

[17]This is a place name for some point near the "Joe Walker Mine."
One informant said it is a "little hill," another that it is a "canyon."

So it didn't snow.

Then Coyote took Rattlesnake[18] back to her house.

D.   McCOWN (SANTOS PHILLIPS)[19]

There was a big meeting at Walker Basin. There were two bears, one white and one with a double head. The mountains from which the white bear came were called *cewüni*.[20] At the meeting they danced and had a ball game with a big ball of heavy, smooth rock. The ball game was played by tossing the ball from hand to hand. The three bears[21] played the game. Coyote came to watch. They made Walker Basin flat by playing this game. The hard rock ball was called *poruba*.[22]

Coyote at the end of the game started dancing. He danced faster and faster. People asked him to dance slower but he said, "I have been all over the world. I must dance fast." There was an artesian well or small lake there. Coyote threw the ball into this. The ball was seen in the water about eighty years ago.[23] Indians around here never see it. Outsiders can see it. The Indians belonged here and can't see.

There are lots of coyotes in Walker Basin. This is because Coyote played there.

All the animals were there. Eagle was boss; he had all the money. Eagle said he would bury all his money after the dance. He did, and it is still buried. Had a round dance with songs. *Ponowatci*, a big jackrabbit, won all the money (*tugubi*),[24] took it all and put it in his belly. He went back to Bakersfield. Coyote tried to kill him. He ran away from Coyote and hid in a hole. Escaped. First ran all over the world. The bears boxed and fought after the dance. The people played dice with walnut shells.

---

[18]This is the only place in the myth where Snake is identified as Rattlesnake. While there are other snakes, to the Kawaiisu, the rattlesnake is *the* snake.

[19]I have recorded this enigmatic myth directly from McCown's notes. Had he prepared them for publication, he might have revised them. Some elements are to be found in other versions, but there are no parallels for others.

[20]Perhaps this is *seewinii*, 'a mountain west of French Meadow'. The stem *see-* means 'white'.

[21]Apparently the 'double head' counts for two bears!

[22]I have recorded the name of the stone as *paribi*; see Setimo Girado's version.

[23]There is a persistent idea that the large rock could be seen in the pond for many years. This statement indicates that it was visible around 1850.

[24]*Tugubi* are 'beads'. They were used as money.

There were three bears in Walker Basin.[26] They went down to Isabella[27] and got a big round rock. They took it back with them and danced and sang and tossed the rock from one to another.

When they were tired of this, they threw the rock down into the earth. It went deep down. The hole became a pond with no bottom. It can be seen today with tule reeds growing around it.

Then the bears turned into real bears. They lost their hands and went up into the mountains.

---

[25]This is the first myth I recorded among the Kawaiisu (1936). Martina Collins was then an aged woman and not inclined to talk much. Undoubtedly she had more to tell, had I been able to communicate with her more effectively.

[26]Both Indians and non-Indians often refer to Walker's Basin. However, most maps designate it as Walker Basin. It is flat and surrounded by mountains.

[27]Isabella is mentioned in several myths. It was a small town located on the main stream of the Kern River, and now gives its name to Lake Isabella, an artificial lake which covers the area.

11. The Origin of the *Pagazozi*[1]

A.

ZIGMOND (EMMA WILLIAMS: ELSIE GARCIA)

Coyote fell into the water of the lake at Lone Pine.[2] It takes all day to walk halfway around the lake. One could see Coyote's hide as he came to the top of the water. Then big worms came out of him and swam to the shore. When they reached the land, they became people. They are the *pagazozi*.

That is why those people eat everything--coyote, dog. They eat the root of sagebrush and filaree grass [*Erodium cicutarium, muutanavɨzivɨ*] that grows around the lake.[3]

---

[1]The Kawaiisu apply *pagazozi* to people to the north, apparently around Owens Lake or Mono Lake. Two possible explanations of the source of the name present themselves. Gayton, who read my manuscript in 1937, commented (personal communication), "The *pakazots* are a kind of queer people, i.e., mythological. They are 'water people'. The Western Mono and also Shoshoneans of the Great Basin believed in them." The presence of large amounts of the puparia of the genus *Ephydra* in Mono Lake was reported by William H. Brewer in 1863. In a letter he notes that "they drift in heaps along the shore. . . . Indians come from far and near to gather them for food. The worms are dried in the sun, the shell rubbed off by hand, when a yellowish kernel remains like a small yellowish grain of rice. This is oily, very nutritious . . . the Indians get fat and sleek" (quoted by J. M. Aldrich 1912:90). Perhaps knowledge about this source of food in Mono Lake might have prompted the origin myth!

[2]This may refer to Owens Lake which is now dry since the water is carried off by the Los Angeles Aqueduct.

[3]The implication is that the Kawaiisu did not eat coyote or dog, though some informants had a contrary opinion. As for filaree (alfilaria), an introduced plant which quickly became naturalized more than a century ago, Emma Williams asserted that horses and cows eat it, but the Kawaiisu do not. Nevertheless, on one occasion, she indicated that "it is eaten raw with salt."

12. The Origin of the Tübatulabal ("South Fork")[1]

A.   ZIGMOND (EMMA WILLIAMS: ELSIE GARCIA)

The "South Fork" were originally Bluejays. That is why they like acorns. They have always lived where they are now.

The story "Bluejay and the Acorns" comes from them.

---

[1]The Tübatulabal are known to the Kawaiisu as the *ɨnɨ'apɨ* but are commonly called "South Fork" because they live principally on the South Fork of the Kern River.

13. Bluejay and the Acorns[1]

A.   ZIGMOND (EMMA WILLIAMS: ELSIE GARCIA)

Bluejay was a South Fork who lived with her husband Eagle in Isabella.[2] Her long tail was her hair in those days. She would tie it up with
tule.

Eagle was a good hunter and went hunting every day. Bluejay would
go out after the acorns of the *saasi* oak.[3] She would get three acorns,
pound them to meal, and put the meal in a bowl. The meal would fill the bowl.
Then she poured in water to remove the bitter taste.[4] She would eat almost
all of the meal and say [sing?] *awasa-ca-ca-ca*[5] as she ate. There would be
a little left which she would cook for the family at home, but they didn't
have enough to eat.

Her mother-in-law didn't like it. She watched as Bluejay took
only three acorns and was getting ready to pound again. She said to Bluejay,
"No wonder there isn't enough to eat. Why don't you take more?" Bluejay
took more, and when she went to pound them, there was so much meal that she
could scarcely handle it. It overflowed the mortar-hole where she was pounding.
Then she went to wash away the bitterness.

Her husband was angry because there wasn't enough to eat. He was
watching her from a hill, but she didn't know that. After the meal was
washed, Bluejay ate as usual and brought home only a little bit more than
before. Her husband came home and told his mother what his wife had done.

----

[1]Emma Williams said that this is a Tübatulabal story, though she
didn't mention this to Cappannari when she told him the same story. Apparently there is a Kawaiisu tradition associating the Tübatulabal with
bluejays. See the "Origin of the Tübatulabal ('South Fork')."

[2]For the location of Isabella, see the notes to "Bears at Walker
Basin."

[3]*Saasi* is Interior Scrub Oak, *Quercus wislizenii* var. *frutescens*.

[4]To be edible, acorn meal had to be leached; i.e., washed with
several pourings of water. Thereafter it could be cooked to any consistency.

[5]The recording is only approximate. No meaning was suggested.

His mother got very angry. So Bluejay went away.

This is why we must use more than three acorns today. If the mother-in-law hadn't forced Bluejay to use more, that would still be enough.[6]

B.   CAPPANNARI[7] (EMMA WILLIAMS: SADIE WILLIAMS)

Eagle and his wife Bluejay lived with Eagle's parents. Bluejay pounded acorns for her in-laws. Every day her husband hunted deer and jack-rabbits for them.

Bluejay had long hair tied in back. Each day she took one acorn to the *pahazi* [bedrock mortar-hole] and pounded it. She put the meal in a sand basin--as we do--and leached it. Then she cooked it and ate it herself. She would bring just one little piece[8] to her mother-in-law.

Each day Bluejay would eat around the edges[9] and take only a little to her mother-in-law. Her husband Eagle watched Bluejay from behind a bush. The mother-in-law said, "It's not enough for us. We always pound one whole seed [acorn]. We always pound one seed for ourselves."[10]

Bluejay got mad.

----

[6]Oak acorns constituted the most important vegetal food source for the Kawaiisu. Seven kinds were available, and the Kawaiisu were familiar with the characteristics of each. The myth does not give the reason why Bluejay preferred *saasi* acorns. Some Kawaiisu informants described *saasi* as "bitter"; others rated it as one of the two "best-tasting" varieties (see *Kawaiisu Ethnobotany*).

[7]Cappannari captioned his version of this myth "Eagle and His Wife Bluejay."

[8]Acorn mush could be cooked to any consistency. A "piece" would imply that the mush was probably allowed to stand and harden after cooking.

[9]This word seems to confirm that the finished product was of a cake-like consistency.

[10]Though Emma Williams was the story-teller for both Cappannari and me, some of the details differ. The differences may be attributed either to the fact that ten years separated the two narrations or to the translations provided by Elsie Garcia and Sadie Williams.

14. Doodle Bug (The Firebrand)

A.

McCOWN (EMMA WILLIAMS)[1]

The *aowoba* [an animal living in little holes in the ground; John Nichols thought it was a tarantula] started out to burn the whole world. He came across South Fork.[2] At *mohat*[3] (Bald Face Mountain) in Kelso Canyon, *tawutc*[4] (Cottontail) took a rock and threw it at *aowoba*. He broke *aowoba*'s knees and then killed him. He took the fire away from *aowoba* and buried it so that it would not burn all the rest of the world. *Aowoba* had obtained the fire at *tipoꞎobidaka*.[5]

B.

ZIGMOND (EMMA WILLIAMS: ELSIE GARCIA)

The Doodle Bug (*aawogobi*)--a little gray bug that makes holes in the ground--was a little man. He was carrying around a stick lit at one end. He came somewhere past Kernville, and burned trees as he went along. There is a mountain, *mahatɨ*,[6] near Kernville that still has no trees on it. He was coming this way to burn around here.

Cottontail (*tavuci*) lived in Kelso Canyon where Isabella Collins now lives.[7] His wife saw Doodle Bug coming. She told her husband. Cottontail

---

[1]It will be noted that Emma Williams told this myth to three anthropologists over a twenty-year period (1929-1949).

[2]He would be coming from the north into Kawaiisu territory.

[3]See *mahatɨ* in Zigmond version.

[4]Cottontail is *tavuci*. Terminal vowels are often omitted in conversation.

[5]This location was not identified.

[6]The mountain may be the same one recorded by McCown as *mohat*. The name, Bald Face Mountain, would seem to fit the description. However, Kernville and Kelso Canyon are at some distance from one another.

[7]The Collins family lived in Kelso Canyon in the 1930s, but by the 1970s only Dewey Collins remained and at another location.

went to watch Doodle Bug coming. He took a big rock and hid himself where Doodle Bug was going to pass. As Doodle Bug passed by, Cottontail hit him with the rock and killed him.

And so Doodle Bug didn't get to burn around here.

C.   CAPPANNARI (EMMA WILLIAMS: SADIE WILLIAMS)

Doodle Bug burned the mountains this side of Mt. Whitney.[8] He walked in this direction carrying fire in a box [?] at the end of a stick slung over his shoulder. He wanted to burn the mountains around here.

Rabbit knew he was coming and was very angry. He waited for him this side of Fred Collins' place.[9] He had a stone in his hand. Rabbit threw the stone and hit Doodle Bug in the knees. Doodle Bug fell down and turned to stone. Rabbit also turned to stone. They are still there right across the creek at Fred Collins' house.

---

[8]Mt. Whitney, the highest mountain in California, is at a considerable distance to the north of Kawaiisu territory.

[9]Apparently Fred Collins still lived in Kelso Canyon in the 1940s. Cappannari worked with the Kawaiisu in the summers from 1947 to 1949, but there is no indication that he was in Kelso Valley or Kelso Canyon. Thus "this side of Fred Collins' place" is not very specific.

15. Coyote Kidnaps Mountain Lion's Sons[1]

A.   ZIGMOND (EMMA WILLIAMS: ELSIE GARCIA)

Mountain Lion lived somewhere around the Piute Rancheria.[2] His wife was Cottontail, and they had twin boys. Mountain Lion was a very good hunter. He went hunting every day. Cottontail gathered sedge roots[3] and would bring home a carrying-basket full.

The grandmother took care of the children while their mother was away. She would rock the cradle[4] until they fell asleep. One day Coyote came along and saw that the children were with their grandmother. He said he was thirsty and asked for water. The grandmother said, "There is some over there in the waterbottle." Coyote said he didn't drink from a waterbottle; he drank from a winnowing basket. He told the old woman to fetch him water from the spring in the winnower. She went and tried to get water with the winnower, but each time she filled it the water ran through. Finally she got mad and came back without water.

When she reached home, Coyote and the boys were gone. She tried to find them, but they were nowhere around. She cried. When the mother came home, the grandmother told her and she cried. As Cottontail cried, she took fire and ashes and put them on her head. The brown spot on the back of cottontails' heads is from the ashes. She tried to track Coyote and the children, but could find no trace of them.

When Mountain Lion came home, they told him. He didn't sleep all

---

[1]Gayton (personal communication 1937) commented as follows: "Coyote Steals Mountain Lion Child"--Yauelmani Yokuts (Newman); Kitanemuk (Kroeber, *Indian Myths of South Central California*); Tübatulabal (C. F. and E. W. Voegelin); Serrano (Benedict).

[2]Piute Rancheria is an area on the side of Piute Mountain where several Kawaiisu households, including that of Emma Williams, were located. By the 1970s it was abandoned.

[3]Sedge roots, *Carex douglasii*, were eaten raw.

[4]The Kawaiisu had two types of cradles. One was oval; the other Y-shaped. The latter could be stuck in the ground and rocked.

night. He knew that Coyote had taken the boys. He left his wife and the grandmother and went to look for them. He tried to track them, and went searching over every mountain. He had a bag of pinyons and a bag of beads hanging at his side. He would cry all day and at night he would lean against a rock and continue to cry. As he cried, he sang: *hoya hoya mahaani* [repeated four times].[5] The streaks on mountain lions' faces are from his tears. In the meantime his wife and the grandmother died.

When Mountain Lion reached the top of a mountain, he would get on a rock and look all around. He did this at every mountain. After many years he came to the Tejon Mountains.[6] He got on a rock on top and looked around. He caught sight of arrows which someone was shooting straight up in the air. He wondered who it was. He came down and went a little distance so that he might see better. As he got near, he saw something moving. He could see boys shooting. He knew they were his children. He said to himself, "At last I have found you."

The little brother told the bigger one that someone was coming.[7] Mountain Lion approached the boys and asked them where they came from and where their house was. The boys had sections of 'cane' [carizzo grass]-- Coyote's 'money'--strung around their necks.[8] Mountain Lion asked many questions and got all the information he could. Then he told them that Coyote was not their real father. They had been taken away when they were very small. The little brother said he thought they were not Coyote's children because they were different from his other children. Mountain Lion told them how Coyote had taken them from their grandmother and how he had been looking for them all these years. He took Coyote's necklaces off their necks and put his beads on them instead. He gave them the pinyons he had been carrying around.

The boys told Mountain Lion about the deer they had killed. He asked them if they were going to take it home. The boys said they would come for it in the morning and Coyote would come with them.

The boys went home, but first they put on Coyote's necklaces. When they got home they told about the deer. Coyote suspected that they had seen someone as he could smell the pinyons they had eaten. Coyote asked if they had eaten anything or seen anyone. They said they had walked under a pinyon tree. Coyote didn't ask further.

They all went to bed. Coyote didn't sleep well. He kept getting up to see if it was morning. He wanted to go after the deer. When it was morning, Coyote woke the boys and told them they should start after the deer. As they came near the place, Coyote sniffed around. He stopped awhile. He

---

[5]No meaning was suggested. The transcription is only approximate.

[6]The Tejon Mountains are to the southwest of the Kawaiisu area, probably in Kitanemuk territory.

[7]It will be recalled that the brothers are first described as twins. Other versions, however, state that one was older than the other.

[8]Coyote's deceitful character is indicated by his use of pieces of common 'cane', *Phragmites australis*, instead of real beads.

knew someone was there. He would stop and say that he could smell someone. The boys told him he was just imagining.

The deer was under a 'black' oak,[9] and Mountain Lion was overhead on a branch of the tree. Coyote began to eat inside the deer carcass. He would eat and look around, take another bite and look around again. Finally he went 'way into the body of the deer and stayed in awhile. Mountain Lion jumped down on the deer and that killed Coyote.

Mountain Lion went to Coyote's house and killed his wife and all his children. He took his two sons and went away. He told the boys he didn't have any home. They would have to roam in the mountains.

And so mountain lions wander about to this day.

B.   CAPPANNARI (EMMA WILLIAMS: SADIE WILLIAMS)[10]

Mountain Lion lived 'way out on the east coast.[11] He was married to Cottontail and had two sons. Every day Mountain Lion went hunting and his wife went after roots. Cottontail went 'way out, near the ocean.[12] Her mother took care of the children while the parents were away. She had a forked cradle[13] lined with tules just like ours, and each day she rocked the children to sleep.

One day, while the parents were away, Coyote came over for a visit. He said to the old woman, "I'm thirsty." She took a cup to get him some water. Coyote said, "I never drink out of a cup. I use a basket." He pointed to a porous basket. So the old woman took the basket and went down to the stream to get him some water. Every time she lifted the basket, the water drained through, and she couldn't get any to stay in it. She kept trying. Finally she came back to the camp. When she got there, Coyote and the two children were gone. Coyote had taken them to his house this side of Tejon Canyon.

The grandmother cried and cried. When Cottontail got home and learned that her children had been stolen, she cried too. She put ashes on the back of her neck, and that is why the backs of cottontails' necks are brown today.

---

[9]*Quercus chrysolepis*--apparently 'black oak' is the local name for the species. It is usually called Canyon Live Oak or Maul Oak in botanical manuals. See *Kawaiisu Ethnobotany.*

[10]Cappannari calls this version "Tiger and Coyote," undoubtedly because Sadie Williams must have translated *tukumɨɨci* 'tiger'. It is not an appropriate name for the American species.

[11]Perhaps this is a typographical error. The Kawaiisu had no familiarity with an "east" coast.

[12]The "ocean" does not usually figure in Kawaiisu tales.

[13]The lower end of the Y-shaped cradle could be stuck in the ground. See footnote 4.

When Mountain Lion got home, he took lots of pinyons and went out across the mountains looking for his sons. He sang a song: *ha no no mai.*[14] He looked everywhere, but he couldn't find them. He looked for a long time. One day, while he was standing on the top of a mountain, he saw some arrows being shot into the air. His sons were hunting deer. Mountain Lion came close and recognized them. He gave them some of his pinyons. Coyote had given the boys pieces of 'cane'[15] and these were strung around their necks. Coyote had told them that they were money,[16] but they were worthless. Mountain Lion broke the necklaces and threw them away. The elder boy said to his brother, "Coyote is really our father," but the younger boy said, "Coyote doesn't look like us. He isn't our father."

Under a tree they found a deer which they had killed. The boys said to Mountain Lion, "Coyote will come after this deer tomorrow." Mountain Lion asked the boys which part of the deer Coyote would eat first. They told him he eats the liver and heart first. The boys went home and told Coyote about the deer. Coyote smelled the pinyons on the boys and asked them why they smelled different. They said they had been under some kind of tree, but Coyote didn't believe them.

Coyote was so anxious to get started that he walked around outside his house all night. In the morning he approached the deer. He was cautious and drew back. Then he slowly came near it again. Mountain Lion was crouched on a branch above the deer. Then Coyote got inside the deer and ate its heart. While he was eating, Mountain Lion sprang down, crushed Coyote inside the deer, and killed him. Then Mountain Lion went to Coyote's house and killed his wife and family. He took his sons and returned home.

C.   CAPPANNARI[17] (MARIE GIRADO: CLARA GIRADO)

There was once an old woman, Gopher,[18] who was taking care of two little boys, the sons of Mountain Lion. Their mother gathered acorns every day and that is why the old woman took care of the boys.

Coyote came there one day. Gopher was there with the boys. Coyote said, "I'm very thirsty." He told the old woman to get him some water. She took a basket which had holes in it. The water drained through it. Coyote said, "Take your time! Put some mud in the basket and then it will hold water." While she was down there, Coyote stole the two boys. He took them home with him, and made them bows and arrows. He had a wife and many other children.

---

[14]Cappannari adds parenthetically "(the rest unrecorded)."

[15]This is carizzo grass, *Phragmites australis.*

[16]Strings of beads (of shell or bone) were used as money. Coyote's "beads" had no value.

[17]Cappannari calls this version "Coyote and Lion" since, in all probability, Clara Girado translated *tukumᵻᵻci* 'Lion' rather than 'Mountain Lion'.

[18]This is the only version in which the old woman is identified.

The parents of the boys were crazy with grief and anger. Mountain Lion was so angry the old woman turned into a gopher and went into her hole.[19] The parents searched the mountains for their children. Mountain Lion was so angry you could see lightning wherever he went. His wife was so tired and worn out he put her inside his belt and carried her that way. Finally she died, so Mountain Lion searched everywhere alone.

Coyote had taught the boys how to hunt. They shot a gray lizard and asked Coyote if it was good to eat. Coyote said, "The ones with little ears--that is, mice and rats--are good to eat so try to shoot them." The boys grew up, and their father continued to search for them.

One day they killed a deer. It was their first deer. That was when their father found them in the mountains. He asked them, "Where have you been staying all this time?" They replied, "Coyote, our father, lives over there." Mountain Lion had some candy made from pine sugar,[20] and he gave some to the boys. Coyote had made them necklaces of cane; Mountain Lion made better ones and put them on the boys.

Mountain Lion said, "Go tell your father to come up and help you skin this deer. I'll be waiting on the limb of this tree." He told the boys that he was their real father and that their mother had died while she was looking for them. The two boys talked about this while they walked home. The elder brother said, "Coyote is our real father." But the younger brother said, "Mountain Lion has hands like ours. None of these people has hands like ours. Mountain Lion is our real father."

Coyote said, "I smell sugar on you. Where did you get it?" The boys said, "There's plenty of those trees up there." "Where did you get those necklaces?" he asked. "We found them," they said. Coyote was frightened.

The boys told Coyote that they had killed a deer. So they all went up there. Coyote saw the deer and looked all around. He smelled Mountain Lion, but he didn't say anything. Instead of showing the boys how to clean the deer, he got right inside the deer and started eating it. He would take a bite and then look around. He kept doing this. Finally he forgot to look. He had his head inside the deer. Mountain Lion jumped down on him. Coyote said, "Let go of me. I have my children to raise." But Mountain Lion killed him. Then Mountain Lion went to Coyote's house and killed his wife and children.

After that Mountain Lion and his sons were always together. They lived in the big hills on the other side of Tehachapi. Mountain Lion never washed his face because his wife died.[21] You can still see the streaks on his face.

---

[19]At this point either Marie or Clara commented: "That's the way those people were--like people until they were frightened and then they turned into animals."

[20]The "sugar pine" is *Pinus lambertiana*. The dried sap was used "like candy."

[21]This may reflect the Kawaiisu-Tübatulabal custom of refraining from washing the face as a sign of mourning.

16. Coyote and Mountain Lion (or Wolf)[1]

A.

ZIGMOND (EMMA WILLIAMS: ELSIE GARCIA)

Coyote was the younger brother, Mountain Lion the elder. The two had a winterhouse in Sand Canyon. Mountain Lion would go hunting every morning. Coyote was lazy and stayed home; he was the cook. Each morning he would go after water with the pitched waterbottle. But he would urinate in the water and it began to smell bad. Mountain Lion noticed the unpleasant odor. Instead of drinking the water brought by Coyote, he would go over the mountain to another spring. As he went he left a trail, and the trail is still to be seen in the rock going over the mountain.

Mountain Lion was a good hunter. He got big game. He would stack the big skins, and the pile of skins is still to be seen in the rock. Coyote was a poor hunter. Whenever he went out to hunt, he brought home only rabbits and other small game. His small pile of little skins is still to be seen in the rock.

The brothers lived there a long time. During the night a bear would pass by, and each morning they could see his tracks. One day they decided to trap the bear. They dug a deep hole, and at the bottom they planted arrows with the points sticking upward. The bear would fall in at night when he couldn't see. After the trap was set, Coyote was anxious to see if the bear was caught. He couldn't sleep, but kept waking up to see if it was morning. He got up very early while his brother was still sleeping. He ran to the trap to see if the bear had been caught. There he was--dead. Coyote hurried to tell his brother. They took the bear out of the hole and began to skin him. Mountain Lion told Coyote to build a fire. Coyote wouldn't do it. "Why should I build a fire?" he said to himself. He didn't build it.

They took out all the insides of the bear, but there was one organ, the $hak^{w}i\check{c}iv\dot{\imath}$,[2] that should have been thrown into the fire. Coyote put it on

---

[1] Gayton's comment (personal communication 1937) on this myth is as follows: "Tale with Shoshonean and Yuman distribution, some general references to it are given in Gayton, *Areal Affiliations of California Folktales*, p. 594, fn. 68. Your version seems most like Walapai."

[2] This is an internal organ, probably the spleen, but the pancreas was also suggested.

the ground. He would go over and touch it and then go back to the skinning.
One time when he tried to touch it, it jumped. He tried to catch it, but it
hopped away. Every time it hopped it said, ""I'm going to tell on you!"
Coyote chased it, but it hopped all the way to Walker Basin where the bear
used to go every day to play with other bears. It told the bears what had
happened.

Next day the bears came to the brothers' house to kill them. The
bears really wanted the kill Mountain Lion [whom they apparently blamed].
Coyote would put on his brother's clothes and go out, but the bears knew it
wasn't Mountain Lion. They kept watching the house. Coyote tried all of
Mountain Lion's clothes, but the bears weren't to be fooled. Mountain Lion
made a flute of elderberry wood[3] and stuck it through the wall of their house.
He and his brother went outside through the flute. He told Coyote not to
look back, but Coyote was curious and looked back. The bears saw Mountain Lion
and shot him. They cut him up into small pieces which they scattered all
over--except the eyes. They took the eyes to Bakersfield where they had a
celebration.

Coyote cried and cried. He looked all over for a tiny piece of his
brother, but he couldn't see any. Finally he found a little spot of blood on
a rock. Coyote took the rock home and put it in a large basket which he
covered. He cried all night. He couldn't sleep. He got up to see if anything had happened in the basket. Suddenly he heard a noise--something like
splashing.[4] He went to look. There was Mountain Lion. Coyote picked him up
and brought him into the house. But Mountain Lion had no eyes.

Coyote killed different animals and brought their eyes to his
brother. Mountain Lion would try them on, but he couldn't see out of them.
Coyote tried the eyes of all the animals, but none of them worked. He knew
that he would have to get back Mountain Lion's own eyes.

Coyote went to Bakersfield. He took the shortest way down,[5] and
ran and ran. He got on a hill to see what was happening. He saw smoke coming out of the houses. An old woman was out getting wood. She would pack it
on her back, carry it away, and put it on her wood pile. She did this all day.
The sun was going down; it was getting late. Coyote thought that this would
be her last load. She tied up the wood and sat down to lift it on to her back.
Coyote came down and stood behind her. Every time she tried to lift the wood,
he would step on it. She couldn't lift it. At last she looked around to see
why it was so heavy. She saw Coyote. "Are you Coyote?" the woman asked.
"No, I am not Coyote," he said. "I've heard of your celebrations and I've
come to watch the dancing."

---

[3]The pithy stems of elderberry, *Sambucus caerulea*, were made into
flutes.

[4]In other versions of the myth it is mentioned that Coyote had
filled the basket with water.

[5]Bakersfield is down in the San Joaquin Valley below the hills
where the Kawaiisu lived.

Coyote asked a lot of questions and the old woman told him everything. She told about the eyes. Coyote asked if she danced. "Yes," she said, "I dance at daybreak." She described how she danced, holding the eyes in her hands. She said that her two little granddaughters would come running to help her as she approached her house with her load of wood. She told Coyote where she slept. Then he killed her. He put her on a flat rock and pounded her so that, when he shook the skin, all the bones and flesh dropped out. Coyote took the skin and put it on. He picked up the wood and carried it to the house. The little girls came running to him. They didn't notice any change. Coyote did everything just as the grandmother had told him. He even walked like her.

Coyote lay with the grandchildren, but he couldn't sleep. He was impatient. He slept a little while and then woke up to see if it was morning. Before dawn he killed the grandchildren.

The dance was going on. They came to take the old woman to dance. Coyote acted as if he were furious because they woke him so early. They gave him the eyes. He danced with vigor and sang *tuwamani* [repeated 6 times].[6] People wondered why the "old woman" was so spry. They asked "her", but "she" didn't answer. They were suspicious, but "she" kept on dancing.

The sun was about to come up. Coyote tightened his hold on the eyes, and ran. He took off the old woman's skin, threw it back at the others, and yelled, "You can dance and celebrate with that!" Everyone left the dance and chased Coyote. When they came up close to him, he would get behind a little bush and become invisible. When they reached the place where they had seen him last, they would find nothing but his tracks. He would be far away, and would call back at them, "What are you doing over there?" They wanted to kill him. They asked the bird *puuciigiigi?ibɨ* to bring snow.[7] Finally they gave up the chase and went back to Bakersfield.

It snowed and snowed. Coyote was high in the mountains. He stayed under a flat rock. Then he got into an acorn cupule and used it as a sled. He said, "Wind, won't you blow?" The wind started blowing and blew the cupule along.

Coyote reached his house. His brother was still alive. Coyote put the eyes on him and he could see. Then they left Sand Canyon, and went to the end of the world. They didn't have any water and couldn't see any. Mountain Lion would kill a rabbit and roast it. At the place where they built the fire, Mountain Lion would stick his bow into the ground. Water came out.[8]

---

[6]The word of the song suggests either *tuwa-* 'son' or *tuwahani-* 'to celebrate', but neither of these was proposed.

[7]This bird, whose name seems to be built on *puucii-* 'star', was reputed to be a weather shaman. One informant identified it as a titmouse and another as a pinyon bird.

[8]A parallel to this episode is to be found in the Chemehuevi myth "The Journeys of Southern Fox"; see Introduction.

Mountain Lion and Coyote remained at the end of the world as two rocks. Whenever there is an earthquake, one of them is moving.

B. ZIGMOND (SETIMO GIRADO)[9]

Coyote and Wolf were brothers. They hunted deer, but Coyote killed nothing. "I am going hunting again," he said. He came home without killing anything.

Coyote urinated in the water at the spring. Wolf wouldn't drink it because it smelled. Wolf was mad at his brother because Coyote urinated in the water. Wolf went looking for another spring. He found one and drank there all the time.

They had a winterhouse. Coyote lay down in it and played his elderberry flute. He called Bear. Bear was angry and made lightning[10] as he went along so they could see where he was. Wolf told Coyote that Bear was angry and was coming. Coyote didn't believe him, but as Bear kept coming closer, Coyote believed him. He went after his quiver and some *tɨavɨ* roots.[11] He dug up the roots and sharpened the ends. Around the house he placed many roots with the points upward. Coyote took his quiver and jumped over the house and over the root-points. "I am going to do that when Bear comes," he said. Wolf said, "Bear is coming closer now." Bear came. Coyote took his quiver and went outside. Bear saw him and chased him. Coyote jumped over the house. Bear followed and jumped too, but he fell down on a point and was killed.

Wolf said, "Skin him—don't throw anything away." Coyote didn't believe him. He threw away the *hak^w̌ičivɨ*.[12] Wolf said, "Why did you throw it away? Go get it!" Coyote went after it, but it jumped to one side. He went after it again, but it jumped farther this time. He chased it. It jumped very far away. The *hak^w̌ičivɨ* said, "I'm going to tell. Many soldiers[13] will come." He went and told. Coyote went home and held his head in his hands. He said, "That *hak^w̌ičivɨ* got away from me." "I told you not to throw it away," said Wolf. "Soldiers are coming. They are very close now."

The soldiers came. They went all around the house. They wanted to kill Wolf. Wolf flew up through the house like a bird. They didn't see him.

---

[9]In their narration of this myth, Setimo Girado and his wife Marie call the brothers Coyote and Wolf. Emma Williams named them Coyote and Mountain Lion.

[10]Lightning is associated with anger in several myths.

[11]*Tɨavɨ* is serviceberry (*Amelanchier pallida*). Arrows are made of its stems but not, to my knowledge, of its roots.

[12]The identity of this internal organ is not clear. Setimo said it is a piece of meat lying over the stomach and not eaten. Both the spleen and the pancreas were suggested. See footnote 2.

[13]"Enemy" would be a more appropriate translation of *tuhugadɨ*, which here must refer to the hostile bears.

"Don't look at me as I fly away," Wolf told Coyote. They shot at him, but they couldn't hit him. Coyote was hiding his face, but finally looked back.[14] Then the soldiers hit Wolf all over, and killed him. They took Wolf away.

Coyote cried because his brother was dead. He lay down by the fire and didn't eat anything. He was hungry. "My brother was a good hunter," he said. He cried some more. He got up in the morning and went down to the place where Wolf had been killed. He looked for him there, but could see nothing. Then he found a small rock with a spot of blood on it. He took the rock home and put it in a basket with water in it. He covered it up and put it away. After three days he went and looked in the basket. His brother was in it. He picked him up. He had no eyes. Wolf said, "Go get my eyes." "All right," said Coyote, "I'll get them." "Many people are using my eyes," said Wolf.

Coyote went there. He was peering down from a hill. The sun had almost set. He saw an old woman getting wood. Coyote asked her where his brother's eyes were. The old woman said, "I'll show you." She told him how they danced at night. They took turns dancing with the eyes in their hands. She was the last to dance. Coyote asked all about it, and she told him. The old woman had two grandsons. Coyote wanted to know what they did. "They play with the eyes like marbles," she said. She went after wood again. Coyote was there. He asked more questions. "When I pack my wood, lie down on top," she said. "All right," said Coyote. When she was bending over to pick up the wood, he jumped on her and killed her.

Coyote skinned the old woman and put on her skin. He packed the wood. It was almost sundown. He carried the wood to where the people were. He acted like an old lady. He had a cane. He went over to the grandsons. People said, "How can the old woman get around so quickly?" "There is nothing wrong with me. I'm going to bed," said Coyote.

It was night. Coyote was in bed. Many people were dancing with Wolf's eyes. Then it was almost daylight. They said, "Call the old woman now. It's almost daylight." Coyote said, "Hand me my cane." He went there and started dancing. "Give the eyes to her," they said. She (he) was the last to get them. He danced with the eyes in his hands. He danced very fast. Suddenly he took off the skin and left it there. He held on to the eyes and ran home. Many people chased him. They nearly caught up with him, but he ran under some sagebrush.[15] They lost him and went on ahead. He yelled at them from far back. They caught up with him again. He went under a rock. They lost him. He yelled from back there again. They went after him. This time he went fast. He had the eyes in his hands.

Coyote went to his brother and put the eyes on him. Wolf could see

---

[14]This description of the situation is confused. It is not clear whether Wolf flew alone or was accompanied by Coyote.

[15]The Kawaiisu word here is *sivapɨ*. While in a general sense it can be called 'sagebrush', it is botanically determined as *Gutierrezia californica*, commonly known as California matchwood.

fine now. Many people came. Wolf said, "Let's go away." "All right," said Coyote. Wolf said, "Don't look back at them." Coyote didn't look back this time. He held his hands by the sides of his eyes. They went from Sand Canyon to Kelso Valley. Wolf said, "They won't kill us again." The soldiers turned into Joshua Trees [*Yucca breviflora*].

The two brothers went to the end of the world. There the *inɨpi*[16] had many doves. Coyote gambled with *inɨpi* for the doves and won. Coyote wanted to bring the doves over here and he did. That is why there are many doves here.

In those seasons when there are no doves, *inɨpi* is winning.[17]

C.   CAPPANNARI (EMMA WILLIAMS: SADIE WILLIAMS)

Coyote and Leopard[18] were brothers. They lived in a brush house above Sand Canyon. Coyote was the younger brother.[19]

They wanted to trap bears. Leopard lay in the house and sang a song.[20] Then he sent Coyote to get some roots[21] to make the trap. Coyote came back with the wrong kind of roots. Leopard kept singing his song and Coyote went out again. But he came back with the wrong roots. The third time he returned with the right roots. Then they made the trap.

There were bear tracks on the ground right near the house and they made the trap there. They dug a big hole and stuck an arrow in it. The bear fell on that arrow and it killed him. The brothers found him in the trap the next morning. They skinned him. Leopard told his brother to build a fire, but Coyote didn't want to. Leopard wanted to cook an appendage[22] from the bear's stomach. Coyote went to get that piece, but it jumped. Coyote chased it and shot at it with his bow. It went clear to the Basin. There were many bears

---

[16]The *inɨpi* is conceived of as spirit, ghost, devil, and has a prominent role in the supernatural world of the Kawaiisu. This episode, however, is not to be found in the other versions of the myth.

[17]Setimo Girado's preoccupation with the gambling theme is to be seen in the atypical tale which I recorded from him entitled "A Gambling Story."

[18]Cappannari called this myth "Coyote and Leopard" on the basis of Sadie Williams' translation. Actually the leopard is the Old World species. The feline of the Western Hemisphere is called mountain lion, cougar, or puma.

[19]Cappannari records the word with the possessive pronoun 'my'—čaka?ini, 'my younger brother'.

[20]At this point Cappannari notes "song not recorded."

[21]The Kawaiisu word is given as *teruba*. More likely it should be *tɨavɨ*, 'serviceberry' (*Amelanchier pallida*) whose stems, not roots, are made into arrows.

[22]In other versions the "appendage" is identified as either the spleen or the pancreas.

there. Every time the thing jumped it said, "*tinyihak.uk* [I am going to the bears]."[23] Coyote didn't follow it to the bears. He stopped by the cattle guard [which is on the road to Walker Pass].[24]

That night the bears came over. They were very angry at the two brothers. Coyote said to his brother, "Do you hear our enemies outside?"[25] The bears wanted to kill Leopard. Coyote went outside the next morning. The bears said, "That's Coyote." Every time he went out, he changed his clothes, but they knew him just the same.[26]

Leopard stuck his flute through the wall of their brush house. He went through the flute to the outside and Coyote followed him. Leopard told his brother he must not look back. Their enemies did not see them go out. Coyote said, "I wonder how many enemies there are." He looked back. Then the bears saw Leopard and killed him. They cut him up in little pieces and tromped him in the dirt. They scattered fragments of his bones. Then they went home.

Coyote returned to his house and cried. Then he went back to the spot where his brother had been killed. He saw nothing in the trampled earth, but finally he noticed a stone with a little blood on it. He brought the stone back to the house and put it in a big basket in the storehouse. He filled the basket with water and covered it with another basket.

Coyote couldn't sleep that night. He went out and looked in the basket several times. Then he slept. When daylight came, he went out and looked in the basket again. His brother was there but he had no eyes. The bears had taken his eyes to Bakersfield. Coyote tried the eyes of many animals on his brother--badger's, owl's, wildcat's, deer's--but none of them worked. Coyote got mad and went to Bakersfield. There the bears were having a feast. Coyote climbed a hill and looked at their houses. He saw an old woman carrying wood for the bears.

It was evening. Coyote crept behind the woman and climbed on the load of wood which she was carrying on her back. At first she didn't notice him. Then she looked back and saw him. "Are you Coyote?" she asked. He replied, "No, I'm from South Fork.[27] I came down to see my friends." Coyote asked her what the bears were doing. She told him that they were having a feast because they had Leopard's eyes. She said that this was her last load

---

[23]The Kawaiisu here does not include the word 'bears'. It is built on the root *tinia-* 'to tell' and seems to mean 'I'm going to tell on you!'

[24]The location is not clear. There may be a confusion between (Walker) Basin and Walker Pass. These are not close together.

[25]*Tuhugadɨ*, apparently derived from *tuhu-* 'black', means 'enemy, murderer'.

[26]The point is that Coyote was trying to draw attention away from Leopard.

[27]The implication is that as a "South Fork" (Tübatulabal), he would not be seeking to recover the eyes.

of wood and that she was returning to her house where she had two grand-daughters. She would dance at the bears' feast and would hold Leopard's eyes when she danced.

Then Coyote killed the old woman. He pounded all her bones on a flat rock. Then he shook her skin and the bones fell out. He put her skin on "like clothes." He picked up the load of wood and carried it into her house. Coyote and the grandchildren went to bed. He slept between the two girls.

Coyote heard singing and dancing. One of the bears came to the house to get the "old woman." He got up and went to the feast with the bear. He sang and danced and juggled Leopard's eyes.[28] The bears noticed how fast he was dancing and accused him of being Coyote. He told them "I'm mad at you for dancing at night. That's why I dance fast." After a little while he took off his "skirt" and ran away with Leopard's eyes. The bears chased him. He came to a female rainmaker--a bird. He told her to make it snow and she did.

Coyote went up to a cave on the mountain. The snow was already very high. He told Northwind to come. Then he climbed into a small hollow object (*povoruba*).[29] Northwind blew and rolled him home. He arrived in the evening and restored his brother's eyes. They decided to go away. They started for the East Coast. When they were in the desert, Leopard made a spring by spitting on a stick and pushing it into the ground. For food they baked jackrabbits. Then they went to the East Coast, far to the end of the world.

They lie at the end of the world on their stomachs. When they move, they cause earthquakes.

D.   CAPPANNARI (MARIE GIRADO: CLARA GIRADO)

Coyote lived up Sand Canyon with his younger brother, Wolf.[30] Wolf was always hunting. Each brother had his own spring and kept its location a secret from the other. One never drank from the spring of the other.[31]

One day Wolf asked Coyote to get some roots to trap bear.[32] Coyote went out to get them. Each time he got the wrong kind. Wolf warned that the bear, the *mupita*,[33] would soon be there. Coyote finally got the right kind of

---

[28]Cappannari adds here "(song)," but none is recorded.

[29]This may be the globular sepal of the bladder sage, *Salazaria mexicana*, *poovoꞋoribɨ*.

[30]The myth, as told by both Marie Girado and Setimo Girado, involves Wolf instead of Mountain Lion.

[31]The reason for the separation is to be found in the other versions.

[32]The name of the plant is given here as *surub*. This appears to be an error. See footnote 21.

[33]This word is undoubtedly the result of a typographical error. A *miitiipi* is any undesirable, and even dangerous, creature.

roots. They sharpened them at one end and placed them around the house so the bear couldn't get in. They knew the bear was coming to kill them.

Wolf was playing his elderberry flute. When the bear came, Coyote leaped over the house. The bear leaped after him, landed on the points, and was killed. Coyote skinned the bear. Wolf told him to destroy every part of the bear. There was a hard part of the liver[34] that Coyote didn't destroy. He told his brother about it. Wolf said, "We are in a bad fix now. It will tell on us. You'd better get it." Coyote went after it, but when he reached it, it jumped. It went toward the east and Coyote couldn't catch it. Each time it made a sound meaning "I'm going to tell!"[35] Wolf said, "Armed people[36] will come for us now." Coyote looked to the east and saw lightning. When they came to the house, Wolf said to his brother, "You must not look at me; don't even glance my way. If you look at me, I'll be killed. I'll be full of arrows. Just walk right through that army." If they didn't look at each other, they would remain invisible to the enemy. But when they left the house, Coyote forgot and looked at his brother. In an instant Wolf was full of arrows. The enemy skinned him and removed his eyes. They took Wolf with them.[37]

Coyote felt so bad he cried. He walked around the spot where his brother had been killed. He found a little piece of rock with blood on it. There was a basket full of water and he placed the stone in it. After three days he heard someone moving around in the basket. It sounded as if someone were taking a bath in there. When he looked in, he saw his brother. But Wolf didn't have any eyes.

Wolf said, "Why do you come to see me? I don't have any eyes. It was your fault that I was killed." Coyote said, "I'll go get your eyes." Coyote knew where the eyes and skin were. He knew that the bears played games in Walker Basin. There he saw an old woman. When Coyote met her, she was gathering wood. He asked her what she was going to use the wood for. She said, "It's for a fire for the dance tonight. They are going to celebrate because they have the eyes and skin of Coyote's brother who was killed not long ago."

Coyote watched every move she made. Soon he knew just how she acted. He asked, "What do you do when you go to your house?" She said, "I walk very slowly. When I get there, I take the wood off my back and rest there a little while. Two little boys come to meet me. They have the eyes. Each day they roll those eyes down the hill. When I get to the dance, it is my job to hold

---

[34]As recorded here, the Kawaiisu word is *harocina*. More accurately, it should be *hak^wičiina*, 'his spleen (or pancreas)'. See footnotes 2 and 12.

[35]Though the recording of the Kawaiisu is garbled, the meaning is clear.

[36]The Kawaiisu word here is clearly *tuhugadɨ* which means 'enemy' or 'murderer' and, by extension, 'soldier'. The last named brings to mind "armed people." See footnotes 13 and 25.

[37]This detail is found in both Girado versions but not in those of Emma Williams.

up the hide and dance around with it." Coyote asked her to show him how she danced. When she finished explaining, Coyote shook her so hard that he shook the bones out of her.

Coyote put her skin on himself. He even put on her little cap. Then he took her load of wood and went down to her house. When he had put his load down, he said, "Hm, hm" [which is the expression used by very old women when they are tired]. He acted just like the old woman. He went to bed and slept at the same time she did. Finally it was time to get up. He got up and went to the dance. The old woman usually danced slowly, but Coyote danced fast. Everyone wondered what was wrong with the old lady. The dance was about over and Coyote took off the old woman's skin. He said, "Hold this and dance with it." Then he ran away with his brother's hide. Those enemies chased him, but they couldn't catch him. He brought the hide to his brother and put it on him. Wolf was still in the water. He had to stay in there until he got his eyes back.

Coyote said, "I have to go back and get your eyes." He knew that the boys played with them. There were times when he could make himself invisible, and he did so now. This time the little boys didn't have the eyes. Coyote asked them where the eyes were and they told him that their mother had them. "She is afraid Coyote will take them from us while we are playing with them." Those two boys were really the sons of two sisters. Coyote asked, "What do you say to your mothers[38] when you ask for those eyes?" They said, "We cry for them." As soon as he learned this, he rubbed them on a rock and shook their bones out. He put on both skins and went to ask for the eyes. The mother said, "No, Coyote might get them." He cried just like the little boys, and she gave him the eyes. He took off the boys' skins and ran away.

The bears came after Coyote again. This time he was having trouble getting away. A large group of enemies were chasing him. When they caught up with him, all they could see where he landed was an old stink bug sitting on the ground. They passed him. Coyote got up and went on. Again the enemies caught up with him. This time he was old feces lying on the ground. Again they passed him. The third time he got home to his brother and put the eyes back. They worked very well. Wolf could see and he came out of the water. "Now we can go to that dance," Coyote said. They went.[39]

---

[38]There seems to be a confusion of numbers here. Was there one mother or two? A few sentences later, the typed copy has "and they gave him the eyes," but "they" is scratched out and a handwritten "she" is substituted.

[39]At this point, according to the other versions, the two brothers go "to the end of the world." Here they go to the bears' dance. It would seem quite unlikely that they would show up among the bears so soon. Marie Girado may well have combined two separate tales. I have therefore placed the final episode of this tale with the parallel myths. See Myth 10.

17. Coyote Marries His Daughter[1]

A.   ZIGMOND (EMMA WILLIAMS: ELSIE GARCIA)

Coyote went hunting rats. He would kill one and eat it.

He had a beautiful daughter whom he loved very much. He thought of
a plan. He took the guts of a rat and tied them around himself. He acted as
if he were hurt. As he came home, he fell down. His son ran to him. Coyote
said that a bear had attacked him. The boy went to tell his mother. Coyote
was singing. He wanted his daughter to come for him. She came and saw that
he was hurt. She tried to carry him into the house, but he was too heavy.[2]
She lifted him, but dropped him again. His wife came and carried him to the
house. She tried to take him in, but he wanted to stay outside. He told them
to burn him.

Coyote told the family that after they had lit the fire to burn him,
they should go to the other side of the mountain where a man lived who looked
just like him. He had a bow and arrow and a net like his. But Coyote didn't
mention his teeth. Coyote said they should give his daughter to this man who
was his friend.

They piled up brush and on top they placed a tule mat. They put
Coyote on the mat together with his knife, net, bow, and arrows. Then they
got their clothes together and were ready to leave. They set fire to the brush
pile; Coyote told them not to look back. As they were going away, his son
looked back. The boy said, "I saw him roll off." The mother was angry because the boy looked back.

As soon as they were out of sight, Coyote ran to the place where he
had told them to go. He got there ahead of them. He made the house look as
if he had lived there a long time. He heard them coming. He went to the door
and asked, "What's the matter?" The family told the story of how his friend

---

[1]See reference in Introduction to Schmerler's "Trickster Marries
His Daughter."

[2]This is an obvious euphemism. Emma and Elsie did not want to tell
me the real reason for her dropping him. See the other versions of the myth.

had been hurt by a bear, and how they had burned him. Coyote's "friend" started to cry. They told him that Coyote had said that his daughter should be given to his friend.

The "friend" said he didn't have anything for them to eat. The mother got seeds which she pounded and they ate them. The "friend" ate, too. As soon as he put some seeds in his mouth, the girls would tickle him, and he laughed. Before night, Coyote said, "I go to bed early." They got ready to go to bed. Coyote said he never slept in the house. It gave him bad dreams.[3]

They lived there quite a long time. The daughter became pregnant.

Sometimes, when Coyote talked to his son, he would forget and call him "son." Then he would correct himself and say "brother-in-law." The boy went hunting rats with his father. The boy suspected that the man was his father and told his mother, but she wouldn't believe it. Coyote and his son would find a rat-nest in a big mound and would poke it to scare a rat out. Coyote was on one side and the boy on the other. Coyote held his mouth open and the rat would jump in. The boy saw in Coyote's teeth four holes which had been drilled by his children. Coyote hadn't said anything about his "friend's" teeth. The boy knew it was his father and ran home. The *inɨpi*[4] took the boy's place at the rats' nest. Coyote asked if the boy was ready. The *inɨpi* whistled. At length Coyote grew suspicious and went around to see. The boy wasn't there.

The boy told his mother, and she told the children that they were going to leave Coyote. The boy had brought a rat.[5] They cooked it and left it under the fire. Then they went up through the sky-hole.

Coyote came home when he found that his son had gone. He ate the rat and looked for the family. He called them but there was no answer. Then he went to drink water. He saw the reflection of the sky in the water, and could see his family going through the sky-hole. He tried to seize them in the water, but he couldn't touch them. Finally he looked up and saw them above. He called them to come back, but they wouldn't. As he yelled, he ran out of breath, and died.

B.   ZIGMOND (EMMA WILLIAMS: SADIE WILLIAMS)[6]

Coyote lived in a winterhouse with his wife *kuwaageʔebi*[7] and four

---

[3]The narrator omits an important detail. Coyote insists on sleeping outside with his daughter. The rest of the family sleep indoors.

[4]As can be seen in another version of the myth, *inɨpi*, the spirit or ghost, exists independent of the body.

[5]In the other versions, Coyote finds the daughter's babe or babes in the fire. Again, it may be the narrator's or translator's sensitivity which prompted the modification here.

[6]Emma told this myth in 1936 with her granddaughter Elsie Garcia as translator. A year later she told it again with her daughter Sadie as translator.

[7]Coyote's wife was described as "a black bird that calls *kuwa kuwa*."

children--two sons and two daughters. He hunted rats, but when he caught one, he ate all of it and never brought anything home.

Once he took the guts of a rat and tied them with a net around his waist so that they hung down in front. He walked very slowly with a cane. The children were playing outside as Coyote came home. His son said, "My father walks slowly." He called his mother and ran to meet his father. Coyote lay down on the ground. The boy asked what the trouble was. "My guts are falling out," said Coyote. "A grizzly bear was eating me." The boy went back to his mother and said, "A bear was eating my father. I'm going to him again."

Coyote was singing "*meevi kuhana paʔičipuuna*,"[8] to tell his son to have his daughter *Pa'ichipuna* come and get him. Coyote said to her, "I can't walk. The bear was eating me. Pack me home." *Pa'ichipuna* tried to carry him on her back with his hands on her shoulders. He was very heavy[9] and she dropped him. Coyote cried in pain. She tried a second time, but dropped him again. He cried out again. *Pa'ichipuna* said, "I don't want to carry him. He's too heavy." She told her mother to carry him. *Kuwage'ebi* packed him into the sunhouse. Coyote cried with pain: "u...u...u.... I'll never get well. Burn me on a pile of brush." They put him on a pile of brush with his knife, arrow, and tule mat by his side. He said, "My friend lives on the other side of the mountain. He looks like me and has a knife, arrow, and mat like mine. After you burn me, move over to my friend and give him *Pa'ichipuna* as a wife." The boys brought fire to one side of the pile. Coyote said, "Go quickly and don't look back or you will see the *inipi*."[10] But the boy looked back and saw Coyote roll off with his knife, arrow, and mat. "He rolled off," said the boy. His mother said, "He told you not to look back. It might be the *inipi*."

They went around the mountain. Coyote ran fast across the mountain, built a winterhouse and a sunhouse, put rabbitskins up around the outside of the winterhouse, and made a spring of water.[11] As the sun went down, the family arrived. Coyote was starting a fire inside. They were talking outside in the sunhouse, but Coyote listened. Coyote said, "What's the matter? Come inside. Sit down here. There is nothing to eat. What's the matter?" *Kuwage'ebi* said, "Your friend Coyote died. We burned him. He told us to come here and live with you." Coyote bowed his head and cried, "*paʔuwi paʔuwi uwi uwi*." His wife went out and brought in some grass seed. Coyote ate it by the handful. The two girls tickled him so that he laughed. "Wait a minute!" he cried out. *Kuwage'ebi* said, "Your friend told us that you should marry *Pa'ichipuna*." Coyote said, "All right," because he wanted to marry his

---

[8]Coyote's song contains the name of his daughter. The other two words were not translated.

[9]As in the previous year, Emma avoids referring to Coyote's attempt to copulate with his daughter piggyback.

[10]To see *inipi* (spirit, ghost) is to court disaster. Here Coyote exploits this fear.

[11]Coyote does everything possible to make his "dwelling" appear old and well-used.

daughter. He sat between the two girls—*Pa'ichipuna* was the younger. They tickled him again. "Ha, ha, ha!" he said. "I'm going to choke. I have had enough. I don't eat much." "Put it away," he said to his "mother-in-law." "Let's go to bed. I always go to bed early, but I don't sleep in here. I sleep in the sunhouse. In here I have bad dreams." He took his mat outside and slept with his daughter. Next morning *Pa'ichipuna* was already big with child.

In the morning Coyote went hunting rats with his "brother-in-law." Coyote was on one side of the rat-house and the boy on the other. The boy poked into the rat nest with a pole. Coyote held his mouth open for the rat to jump in. Sometimes the rat got away and climbed a tree. Coyote said, "The rat is running to you, my son—I mean, my brother-in-law." Coyote opened his mouth and the boy saw his tooth. He saw four holes in the tooth. Each of his children had drilled a hole. The boy recognized his father and ran home. "Mother," he said, "he is our father. He has four holes in his tooth." She said, "*hanageepɨ yovinɨwɨgadɨ*!"[12] The mother squeezed the babies out of her daughter. There were many of them. The family roasted them, left them by the fire in the sunhouse, and went away. They left tracks near the sunhouse and went up into the sky.

The *ɨnɨpi* took the place of the boy at the rat-house, and poked into it with the pole. After awhile Coyote saw that his son was not there. He ran home, but found that the family had gone. He took the babes out of the fire, removed their heads, and ate them. He kept looking around while he was eating. He went to the stream to drink some water. As he leaned over, he saw the reflection of the water. He tried to catch them in his hands. Then he looked up and caught sight of them in the sky. He yelled, "Come back!" but they only smiled at him. He kept yelling and running around. Finally he was exhausted and out of breath. He died.

The family became five stars which may be seen in the morning sky in winter.[13]

B.   ZIGMOND (SETIMO GIRADO)

Coyote had a house and he lived there with his wife, two daughters, and a son. His mother-in-law lived with them also. He said, "I'm going out in the hills to get something to eat." His mother-in-law went along. Coyote loved his mother-in-law. They went into a cave where acorns and chia were stored.

It was night. They lay down. The mother-in-law went to sleep. When

---

[12]These two Kawaiisu words express a strong denunciation. The first word combines *hana* 'who?' and *-geepɨ* 'deceased, discarded' and may be freely translated 'a nobody'. The meaning of the second word is not clear. There may be an error in the recording. In any case, Emma thought that the total meaning is something like "Shame! Shame!"

[13]The stars apparently form the Pleiades.

she was asleep, Coyote got up, scratched on the wall of the cave with his nails, and growled. Then he lay down quickly and pretended to be asleep. The mother-in-law woke up frightened. "Two more times," said Coyote. He got up and looked at his mother-in-law. He scratched and growled. Then he pulled his rabbitskin blanket over him and pretended to be asleep. The mother-in-law got up frightened and lay close to Coyote. Coyote said, "One more time." He scratched and growled. The mother-in-law got up frightened. Coyote wanted to copulate with her. He climbed on. In one night she was already pregnant. The next morning they were returning home. Coyote picked up his bow and arrow and shot his mother-in-law. He killed her.[14]

Coyote was ashamed. He flew away high in the air. As he came down, he hurt his knee on a rock. When he reached home, he called loudly for his daughter. "Come and get me," he said. "Pack me home." "No," she said, "you're too heavy." Coyote told her that soldiers had killed her grandmother. "Tell your mother to come and get me," he said. "Look, my knee is broken," he said to his wife. She packed him home. "How did it get broken?" she asked. "Soldiers were shooting at me, but they didn't hit me. I jumped over and hurt my knee. Your mother was killed," he said.

Coyote was sick. "When I die, burn me. Put my knife and net at my side. Burn me in the house. Don't look back or you may see *inɨpi* come out," said Coyote. "Over on the other side of the mountain lives my friend. He looks like me. He has a scar like mine, and his knee is hurt. Go to him. Maybe he will marry one of our daughters, and he will bring home deer and rabbits and rats." They burned him, but he cut the net off of himself with his knife. The boy looked back and said, "There is my father." His mother said, "You saw the *inɨpi*."

Coyote ran over the mountain and built an old house. There were ashes around as if he had lived there a long time. He looked out and saw smoke. "There's my friend burning," he said. His wife and daughters and son came to him. "Your friend is no more," said the wife. She cried and Coyote cried. "I knew long ago that he was going to die," he said. "What did my friend say?" The wife said, "He told us that you can stay with one of his daughters." He went to sleep with a daughter.

In the morning he said to his son, "Let's go and hunt rats." They set fire to the rats' nest and stood on either side to shoot the rat as it came out. The rat came out and Coyote said, "My son—oh, I mean, my brother-in-law!" The boy looked at him. "He is my father," he thought. He spat on a rock and ran to tell his mother. Coyote was still on the other side of the nest. When he talked, the spit answered. "That's my father," the boy told his mother. She said, "We will kill him."

---

[14]Setimo Girado and his wife Marie, who told this myth about ten years apart (1937 and about 1948, respectively), both use the mother-in-law episode as preliminary to the main theme of Coyote and his daughter. The same episode is to be found in the mythology of the Tübatulabal (Voegelin 1935:211) and of the Chemehuevi (Laird 1974:221, also 1977:50-51).

Coyote came home hungry. His wife pounded bunchgrass seed [*naara, Melica imperfecta*] and gave it to him to eat. His daughters tickled him. "Wait!" he said. He opened his mouth wide and they put in a handful of the *naara.* "Water!" he said. They put more seed in his mouth. He choked and died.[15]

"Now we killed him," said his wife. "He is no more."

C.   McCOWN (JOHN NICHOLS)

One day Coyote killed a rat. He took the guts out and tied them around himself. This was to make it look as if he had been wounded by a bear. The guts were tied on with string. Coyote's son went to tell his mother that a bear had hurt Coyote. Her name was *kuarub.*[16] She sent their oldest daughter to pick up her father and carry him home. Coyote insisted that his youngest daughter, *paiutca puna,*[17] should carry him. She came to pick him up, but he tried to copulate with her piggyback, so she threw him down. This happened three times. She left him and told her mother to go after him. The old woman packed him into the house. She and the girls decided to burn Coyote.[18] They thought he would die anyway.

They made a big pile of brush and tules outside the house. Coyote said he had a friend who looked just like him. "Everything I have my friend has,"[19] Coyote said. He told the family to go over to his friend's house and stay there. So they set fire to the pile of brush and tules. As they were leaving, Coyote said, "Don't look back. You will see an *ünüp.*"[20] But Coyote's son looked back and saw his father roll off the brush. "Oh, mother, father has rolled off," he said.

The family went around the hill as Coyote had told them to do. He ran over the hill as fast as he could. He had a "dog" of white brush; it was

_____

[15]Both Setimo and Marie Girado use the seed-eating episode as the means by which Coyote dies. In Emma Williams' narrative, this element is treated as a kind of harmless by-play. Both the seed-stuffing and the transformation of the family into a star constellation appear to be valid endings of the tale. Unfortunately the changes in the plot cannot be traced.

[16]Coyote's wife, more correctly transcribed *kuwaage?ebi,* was a bird described by John Nichols as a "little brush bird with red eyes."

[17]The younger daughter's name was *pa?ičipuuna,* derived from *pa?yɨci* 'kangaroo-rat'.

[18]Since the "plot" is Coyote's, it is not likely that the family would make the decision to burn him!

[19]McCown adds a comment here: "(i.e., their features were identical)."

[20]The *inɨpi* 'spirit, ghost' may remain even after the body has departed. There is a similar situation in one of the versions of the "Race from Victorville to Koso Hot Springs" myth.

called *cenub*.[21] Coyote reached the "friend's" house first. The girls found him there when they arrived. He cried when he told him that their father had died, but he was just fooling them. He said to *kuarub*, "Coyote told me to ask for your youngest daughter for a wife." Finally Coyote's wife agreed to this. There was a pot of food which was pounded up, and he fed them. When night came, Coyote took the young girl outside and slept with her. The others he left inside the house.

Coyote got up in the morning and told his son that they would go rat-hunting. The boy went with his father and poked a long stick into the rats' nests. Coyote stood on the other side and ate the rats as they ran out of the nest. He never killed any of them.[22] The two hunted a long time. Coyote ate lots of rats, but didn't kill any. Finally the boy became suspicious since no rats were being killed. He looked under the nest and watched Coyote. He saw Coyote catch and eat a rat. He noticed that there were four holes in Coyote's mouth.[23] He ran away and told his mother that the "friend" was old man Coyote. His mother said, "That's right. He must be Coyote."

The youngest daughter had already given birth to Coyote's baby. The mother and daughter got mad. They put the baby in the fire under the ashes. The baby's spirit went out of the smoke-hole and into the sky.[24] It became a star. The family ran away and went up into the sky. They form *tcaniu*, a cluster of stars in the form of a circle [Pleiades?].[25]

Coyote returned. He found something in the fire. He thought it was food and ate it. Then he followed the track left by the family and came to the river. He looked into the water and saw the stars. He thought they were in the water and called for them. He hollered himself to death.

D.   CAPPANNARI[26] (EMMA WILLIAMS: SADIE WILLIAMS)

Coyote lived with his family in a brush house. He had two daughters and a son. One day Coyote was out alone hunting rats. When he killed some

---

[21]The name of Coyote's "dog," more properly transcribed *seenabɨ*, is identical with that of the plant Silky California Broom (*Lotus procumbens*). It is therefore reasonable to assume that the plant is Coyote's dog.

[22]Since the rats jump directly into Coyote's mouth and are immediately eaten, they are not "killed" in the sense of being collected and taken home as food.

[23]The holes were apparently drilled by the children but no explanation of the reason or the process is given.

[24]This element is not to be found in the other versions of the myth.

[25]Though McCown is uncertain as to the identity of the cluster of stars, his surmise is probably correct. A more accurate transcription is *caniyoʔovɨ*.

[26]Cappannari calls this version of the myth "Coyote and the Big Dipper" on the assumption that the constellation into which the family is transformed in the sky is the Big Dipper.

rats, he took out their guts and tied them around his abdomen. His son met him as he was returning. Coyote said, "A bear has just killed your father. Go get your younger sister and tell her to come and help me." He had the guts wrapped around his belly with a net. The daughter came and put him on her back. Coyote asked her to lower him a little. He wanted to have intercourse with her, but she wouldn't let him. Finally his wife came and carried him home. She let him copulate with her.

Coyote said, "You must burn me. Then go over to the other side of the mountain and you will see someone who looks like me. He has the same knife and the same clothes. Give my younger daughter to that man."

The family put his bow and arrow beside him, and built the fire on one side of him, as he told them, and not all around. "When you light it, start around the mountain and don't look back or you might see *inɨpi*,"[27] he said. So they lit the fire and started for the other side of the mountain. When they had gone a little way, the boy looked back and said, "Father has rolled off the fire." His mother said, "You mustn't look back. You might see an *inɨpi*."

When they were out of sight, Coyote left and ran to the other side of the mountain. He built a house and made it look old. Soon the wife and family came along and saw the house. Coyote asked them what had happened. The wife said, "Your friend has died and we have burned him." Coyote cried, "*pa oi oi oi*."[28] Then he asked, "What did he tell you?" The wife said, "He told us to come here and you are to marry our youngest daughter." Then she prepared lunch for him. She pounded seeds. His two daughters tickled him while he was eating, and he laughed, "Ha, ha, ha, ha."

Coyote said, "I always sleep outside. I dream badly when I sleep in the house." So he took the younger daughter and slept with her outside in the bushes. The next morning the girl's belly was already big.

Coyote went out to hunt rabbits[29] with his "brother-in-law." As the boy poked a rat hole with his stick, Coyote opened his mouth to eat them. The boy looked in his mouth and saw the three holes which his father had in his teeth.[30] The children had made the holes. Coyote said, "Hey, son, oh excuse me, brother-in-law." The boy went home and told his mother that the "friend" was really his father Coyote.

They squeezed the girl's belly and the babies came out. They baked the babies and then went away in the sky. There they became the Big Dipper.[31]

---

[27]At this point Cappannari adds parenthetically: "(his ghost)."

[28]Cappannari adds parenthetically: "(musically)"—that is, in the narrative Coyote's weeping was sung.

[29]This must have been recorded in error. As seen in the next line, rats, not rabbits were hunted.

[30]Some versions mention four holes. The difference is to be accounted for by the number of children Coyote had.

[31]While not all the informants identified the constellation as the

Coyote came home and tracked them, but the tracks ended outside the door. While he walked around looking for the family, he ate the baked babies. He got thirsty and went to the spring for a drink. He saw his wife and children in the water and reached for them. But they weren't there. Then he looked up at the sky and called them to come back. They didn't and he died.

E. CAPPANNARI (MARIE GIRADO: CLARA GIRADO)[32]

Coyote took his mother-in-law up to a cave and kept her there all night. They had gone to the cave to get something [in storage?]. They were just going to bed. Coyote said to his mother-in-law, "Listen to me carefully. This cave is haunted. It makes some kind of noise." They had their bedding at opposite sides of the cave. It was dark. Coyote took a stick and rubbed it against the ceiling of the cave. The mother-in-law jumped up and came to Coyote's bed. Coyote said, "Don't be alarmed. It only does that three times. Get back to your own bed. This isn't right."

Coyote made the noise a second time, and the same thing happened. He said, "It's only going to do that once more." So she got back into her own bed.

The third time he made lots of noise. The mother-in-law jumped up and got under his covers. Coyote said nothing this time, and she stayed there. They never slept. They had intercourse all night long. When morning came, she was already big with child. Coyote didn't like that. He didn't mean for her to get pregnant. He was angry and killed her with his bow and arrow.

After he killed her, he jumped up to run away. He didn't want to get caught. As he jumped, he hurt his knee against a rock. It was the first time he knew that his knee-cap could move around. He stayed where he was and shouted for his daughters to come. The elder daughter came up the canyon and asked her father what was wrong. He said, "My knees were broken. I can't walk." He showed her how his knee-cap moved around. He said, "Put me on your back and carry me home." She put him there, but he said, "No, that's too far up; a little lower would be just fine." He started to have intercourse with her, but she dropped him. Coyote said, "Tell your younger sister to come for me." So the younger daughter came. He tried the same thing with her. She was frightened and dropped him. He said, "Tell your mother to come and get me. She will surely pack me home." His wife came. He got on her back and said, "A little lower." He started having intercourse with her and continued

---

Pleiades, it seems less likely that the Big Dipper was the one meant. The latter, as usually delineated, consists of seven stars and is generally considered a segment of a larger grouping, Ursa Major—the Big Bear. It may well be that, before contact with the Caucasians, the Big Dipper was not conceived of by the Kawaiisu as a distinct entity.

[32]Marie Girado's version of the myth parallels that of her husband Setimo (told about ten years earlier) in that both the beginnings and endings are the same. It must be assumed that these versions belong to a line of tradition which differs from the one reflected in Emma Williams' account. Cappannari calls Marie Girado's tale "Coyote and His Mother-in-Law," but he thus neglects the central plot—Coyote and his daughter.

all the way down. She didn't mind at all and brought him home.

Later, Coyote said to his daughters, "I am very sick. I'm going to
die. Your grandmother has many holes in her body. Our enemies[33] did that.
I escaped, but I'm going to die. I don't want to die like this. Tie me in a
net and put a knife by me. Then burn the house and I'll be burned with it.
I have a brother who looks just like me. He has an old shack with ashes in the
front yard. He'll take care of you for me. When you start the fire, don't
look back. You might see my spirit and that would be bad."[34]

They started the fire on the outside, but the house was soon burning.[35] Coyote cut the net and was just coming outside the house when the
little boy looked back. "Papa's coming out," he said. His mother said, "You
must not look back. You have already seen his spirit (*inɨpi*)." Coyote took
off and went to the place to which he had directed his family. He built a
brush house and made it look old. The family came there. The old woman said,
"Your brother just died." Coyote cried and cried, "Oh my brother!" The old
woman said that Coyote told them to live with his brother who would take care
of them and marry one of the girls. "That's fine," he said. He slept with
the oldest girl.[36]

In the morning Coyote went out hunting with his younger son. While
they were hunting, Coyote would say, "My son," and then he would say, "No,
my brother-in-law."[37] They were digging roots.[38] He kept saying, "Towards
you, my son--oh, I mean my brother-in-law." The little boy became suspicious
and looked at his father's teeth. He thought, "They look just like my father's
teeth." When they got home, the boy told them what his father had called him.
Each day when they went out Coyote made the same mistake.

The mother and daughter were pounding bunchgrass seeds [*naara(bɨ)*,
Melica imperfecta]. They pounded them until they were like powder. That night,
when Coyote came home, he sat between the girls. He teased them, and they
were giggling. They started eating the pounded seeds. Coyote filled his
mouth and the girls tickled him to make him choke. He asked for water, but
they put more of the seeds in his mouth. "Water!" he said, "I'm dying!" They
wouldn't give him any, and he choked to death.

---

[33]The Kawaiisu word *tuhugadɨ* apparently derives from *tuhu-* 'black'.
It is variously translated 'enemy, murderer, soldier'. The basis for the
derivation is not clear.

[34]No explanation is given as to why seeing the *inɨpi* is "bad." The
Kawaiisu regarded it as an unlucky omen.

[35]Usually Coyote is described as being burned outside the house.
However, houses were made of brush and thus could easily catch fire.

[36]According to other versions, Coyote sleeps with the younger daughter.

[37]If this is Coyote's brother, then he would also be the boy's
uncle.

[38]They were hunting rats, as the subsequent sentences imply - not
digging roots.

18. Coyote and His Pregnant Daughter

A.

ZIGMOND (SETIMO GIRADO)

Coyote slept with his daughter. She became pregnant and sick. Coyote went for Hummingbird, the curing shaman. Hummingbird doctored the girl. He asked, "How did she get sick?" He found out and sang, "*muutanarugeeni muutanarugeeni tamiyudɨniastɨgɨrɨ.*"[1]

The doctor accused Coyote of being the one. Coyote got angry and said, "No, it isn't mine."

B.

CAPPANNARI

Coyote had made his daughter pregnant but he pretended she was just sick. He called Hummingbird, who was the first doctor, to come and cure her. While Hummingbird was singing, Coyote pretended to be asleep. He "woke up" and said he hadn't heard the song. So Hummingbird sang it again and again. Coyote wanted people to think that his daughter was ill and not that she was going to have his baby. He paid Hummingbird with awls. Those awls are Hummingbird's bill now.

Coyote called another doctor--Mallard.[2] While Mallard sang, Coyote pretended to be asleep. He "woke up" and said he hadn't heard the song. So Mallard sang it again and again. The next morning Coyote paid Mallard with red pitch (the gummy substance found on both sagebrush [*Artemisia tridentata*] and creosote bush [*Larrea tridentata*]; it is used to fashion handles for awls and knives). Mallard put the pitch on his nose and now he has a white [?] spot there.

---

[1]The recording of these words must be regarded as only approximate. No translation was provided, but the first word (repeated) is apparently derived from *muutanapiži* 'hummingbird'.

[2]Though the Kawaiisu word *kurasɨni* (*kuravi* 'neck') was rendered 'swan' by the interpreter, it is probabably 'mallard'. Swans are not native to the area.

19. Coyote and the Canada Geese[1] (Penis Baby)

A.
ZIGMOND (SETIMO GIRADO)

There were five young girls who were Canada Geese. Coyote went to visit them. He wanted to pass as a girl so he made himself bangs and put on breasts of mud. He held his penis in his hands like a baby. The girls wanted to hold the baby. They asked for it. Coyote said, "Oh, no!" They pinched the baby. It cried just like a baby.

At night Coyote got in bed with the girls. In the morning they were all pregnant.

Coyote went hunting.[2] The girls gave birth to babies. They made a big fire, put the babies in the fire and covered them with dirt. Then they flew up into the sky and looked down. They saw Coyote coming to the house to look for them. He found the babies and ate them all.

Coyote was full. He went to the water to drink. He saw the reflection of the girls in the water. They were smiling down at him. He wanted to come up to them. They linked their wings together, reached down to him, and began to bring him up. When he was half-way up, he said, "Pull me all the way up." When he was almost at the top, they shook him off and let him fall to the ground. He was killed.

B.
CAPPANNARI (MARIE GIRADO?)

Three girls (Canada Geese) lived together. Coyote wanted to have those girls. He pretended to be a woman and went to visit them. He had a "baby" wrapped in his arms. It was really his long penis. He folded it and wrapped it with buckskin. The girls said, "Let us see your baby." Coyote said, "No, you can't see it. It's too wild." He would squeeze it and it made strange noises. He kept pretending to play with his baby because he was itching to get those girls.

---

[1]In both versions of this myth, *orokopi* was rendered 'crane'.
Setimo Girado said that the birds are to be seen flying together in V-formation in the spring, and an informant identified them as Canada geese in the 1970s. Cranes are not recorded for the Sierra Nevada area.

[2]From this point the myth duplicates "Coyote Marries His Daughter."

91

Coyote stayed there that night and took turns with each one. They all became pregnant. The next day their babies were born. They burned them in hot coals and buried them. Then the three girls went up into the sky.

Coyote came around again and looked for them. He saw something buried in the ground. He dug up the babies and ate them. After he finished eating, he went to drink some water. It was night. He looked in the water and saw the reflection of the three girls. He told the girls to come down. They were smiling, but they wouldn't come down. Then they made a cord from their feathers and told Coyote to come up. He started climbing up the cord. Just as he was about at the top, they let go of the cord and down he came.

20. Coyote and the Red Racer[1] (Bungling Host)

A.   <u>ZIGMOND (EMMA WILLIAMS: ELSIE GARCIA)</u>

Red Racer had a winter-house; he also had a sun-house.[2] Coyote came for a visit, and Red Racer saw him coming around the sun-house. Red Racer was sitting by the fire in the winter-house and invited Coyote to come in and sit down. They sat and talked until noon. Red Racer said, "I don't have anything to eat in the house." He took his bow and arrow and went outside to a field of desert-thorn.[3] Coyote was very inquisitive; he peeked at Red Racer through the door. Red Racer put down his bow and arrow, and got under a desert-thorn bush; "*hudukuguuri*,"[4] he said. He moved back and forth, and scraped meat off his back. Picking up the meat, he brought it into the house. As he came in, Coyote sat back as if he hadn't been watching.

Red Racer set the meat down in front of Coyote and told him to help himself and roast some. He said that whenever he was hungry, he got meat that way. Coyote took his knife and cut off a little piece. Red Racer said, "Take more." Coyote said he didn't eat much, but Red Racer told him to take the meat home with him. Coyote did, but before leaving he invited Red Racer to visit him and promised to give him a star-shirt.[5] On the way home Coyote ate the meat piece by piece so that all of it was gone by the time he reached home.

It was a few days later when Red Racer returned the visit. Coyote told his children to stay outside and watch for a visitor who would be coming along. When they saw Red Racer, they ran to tell Coyote, "A Tübatulabal[6] is

---

[1]This myth parallels an episode in a Chemehuevi myth related by Laird (1976:162-8). The incident is discussed in the Introduction.

[2]*Tomokahni*, literally 'winter-house', was actually the usual living house; *tavikahni* 'sun-house' is a brush enclosure at times perhaps synonymous with *havakahni* 'shade-house'.

[3]Desert-thorn, *Lycium cooperi*, is a thorny, densely-branched shrub.

[4]*Hu(n)dukuvi* is the muscle along the sides of the backbone.

[5]See the note on "star-shirt" in the "Coyote and Crow" myth.

[6]Tübatulabal is the name of the tribe adjacent to the Kawaiisu to the north. No reason is given for using the term here, but there was a friendly relationship between the two tribes.

coming!" Each child repeated the same thing.

Coyote and Red Racer talked until noon. Coyote said that he didn't have anything to eat at home. He took his bow and arrow and went out to a field of desert-thorn bushes. Red Racer knew very well what Coyote was going to do, but he didn't pay any attention. He just sat and talked with Coyote's wife.[7]

Coyote went under a bush and tried to scrape meat off his back, but the thorns hurt him and he jumped away crying, "*kikik*!" He tried again and again. The thorns caught in his fur and scratched him all up. He didn't get any meat. Finally, he gave up and started back to his house, bleeding. He died at the door.

Coyote's wife asked Red Racer if that was what he had done when Coyote had visited him. Red Racer said, "Yes" and told how he had given Coyote meat to take home. "He never brought anything home," said the wife. Red Racer asked about the star-shirt. The wife said there wasn't any.

B.   ZIGMOND (REFUGIA WILLIAMS)[8]

Coyote went visiting at the winter-house of Snake [a desert snake, gray, darker toward the head].[9] Snake told Coyote to sit down. Snake went out in his yard. There was a bush (*canavɨ*)[10] which has stiff little thorns on it. Snake went back and forth under the bush to scrape meat off himself for his guest. He kept saying, "*hundukuguur*"[11] [meat or loin from the back]. Then he brought the meat in to Coyote and said, "Here, cook it and eat it." Coyote cooked it and ate it. Coyote invited Snake to visit him. Then he went home.

A long time after, Snake went to visit Coyote. Coyote told him to sit down. Coyote went out in the yard. He went back and forth under the bush. Thus he killed himself.

_____

[7]Coyote's wife is *kuwaageʔebi*, an unidentified bird.

[8]Refugia Williams is the best known of Kawaiisu women. The "gold-seeker," Hamp Williams, married her when she was a young girl, but when he "struck it rich," she preferred to live in her traditional ways. Ardis M. Walker devotes a chapter to her in his *The Rough and the Righteous of the Kern River Diggins* (1971). I met her a year or two before she died, and under the protective eye of two daughters, she talked with me briefly (1937). The condensed form of this tale may be attributed to her failing memory.

[9]I do not know whether the description helps to identify the snake as a red racer. Refugia called it simply "snake."

[10]The Kawaiisu name of the bush clearly identifies it as *Lycium cooperi*, the desert-thorn bush.

[11]I here retain the '*n*' before '*d*'. Like '*m*' before '*b*', it gradually disappeared from the language.

King Snake[12] lived in a brush house.[13] One day Coyote visited him. King Snake said, "I have nothing to eat." Coyote said, "I don't eat much." They talked a little while. King Snake went outside to some bushes with "little stickers"[14] on them. Coyote watched King Snake crawling under the bushes. King Snake came out with meat on his back. Coyote cooked the meat and saved some for his children. He told King Snake to come to his house and he would give him his white shirt.[15]

The next day King Snake visited Coyote. They talked a little while and then Coyote went outside. He crawled under the same kind of bushes that King Snake had crawled under. But he didn't get any meat. He just got scratched and died.

King Snake asked Coyote's wife for his white shirt. She said, "He ain't got nothing."[16]

---

[12]Kawaiisu *kaaʔyagara* is usually identified as 'king snake'. Here the Kawaiisu word is *wiigara*.

[13]Sadie frequently translates *tomokahni* 'bush house', but the construction is of brush tightly bound together with poles and cord. Therefore I have used the term 'brush house' here and elsewhere.

[14]"Little stickers" does not adequately describe the sharp, hard thorns characteristic of the desert-thorn bush.

[15]See note on "star-shirt" appended to the "Coyote and Crow" myth.

[16]It is my impression that Cappannari is here reflecting the spirit, but not the words, of the myth text.

21. Coyote and Crow[1] (Bungling Host)

A.

ZIGMOND (EMMA WILLIAMS: ELSIE GARCIA)

Coyote came to visit Crow. When he entered the house, Crow was seated and told Coyote to sit down. They talked together until noon. Crow said, "I can't give you much to eat." He thought of how he might get some food for his guest. He took his bow and arrow and some fire, and went out. There were grass and brush growing near his house. These he burned in a circle to trap rabbits and rats. Crow was in the middle of the circle, and as the animals ran toward him, he killed them. He killed many rabbits and rats. When the fire got close to him, he took all the dead animals and jumped over the fire.

Coyote was peeking out to see what Crow was doing. Crow roasted all the animals and gave them to Coyote. Crow told Coyote to eat all he wanted. Coyote said, "I don't eat much, but I'll take the rest home to my children." Crow agreed to this. Before he left, Coyote invited Crow to visit him. "When you come," he said, "I'll give you a star shirt."[2]

Coyote put all the animals in his net and started home, but as he went along he ate them one by one until there was none left when he reached home. He told his children to stay outside and watch. "We are going to have company," he said. "You will see him coming." And so they went outside and played. They saw Crow coming. One by one, from the oldest to the youngest, they ran to Coyote and told him, "A Tübatulabal is coming!"[3]

Coyote told Crow to come in and sit down. They talked until noon. There wasn't anything to eat. Coyote took his bow and arrow and some fire and went out. He burnt brush in a circle. He shot the animals as they appeared,

---

[1]Gayton (personal communication 1937) comments as follows: "Familiar 'Bungling Host' type of faulty imitation (Cf. Lowie 1924:19-21, 23, 171, for examples from the Basin)."

[2]The "star shirt," *puuciinaroʔo*, combines two words, *puuciivɨ* 'star' and *naroʔo* 'shirt'. It is apparently a product of Coyote's imagination and never appears except in invitations to his prospective guests.

[3]No reason is suggested for calling Crow a Tübatulabal. Perhaps it is because the Tübatulabal were familiar and friendly neighbors.

but he didn't kill many. He waited until the fire was too close, and when he jumped, he jumped into the fire and was burned to death.

Coyote's wife *kuwaage?ebi* (a small bird with red eyes and a red breast)[4] asked Crow if he had done the same thing. Crow said "yes" and told how he had given Coyote meat which Coyote hadn't eaten but said he would take home. "Didn't he bring the meat home?" Crow asked. "No," said *kuwaage?ebi*, "he never brought home anything good to eat." Crow asked about the star shirt. The wife said he didn't have any. Coyote had just told him that to make him come.

Then Crow went home.

B. CAPPANNARI (EMMA WILLIAMS: SADIE WILLIAMS)

One day Crow was out hunting. He built a big fire around himself. The fire killed rabbits and rats.[5] He gathered the game and jumped out of the fire. Then he roasted the game in the coals left by the fire. As he was eating, Coyote came along[6] and Crow gave him some meat. Coyote saved some to take home to his children. He invited Crow to come over the next day and promised to give him his white shirt (*pučinaro*).[7] As Coyote walked home, he ate all of the meat that he was going to give his children.

The next day Crow came over. Coyote's children saw him coming and said, "Daddy, Crow is coming." Coyote said, "Oh, I'm busy!" Crow came in. Coyote said, "I have nothing to eat." He went out with his bow and arrow and burned the bushes like Crow did. But he didn't get as much game as Crow had. When the circle of fire came up to him, he burned to death.

Crow said to Coyote's wife, "I came to get Coyote's white shirt." The wife said, "He doesn't have any white shirt."

C. CAPPANNARI (MARIE GIRADO: CLARA GIRADO)

Coyote went to visit Crow. When Coyote arrived, he saw that Crow was catching game. He was burning grass in a big circle and causing the game to run to the center. Coyote watched Crow collect the game in his bag. Then Crow flew straight up with his bag.

Coyote said to Crow, "Tomorrow I want you to come over and visit

---

[4]This bird was not identified.

[5]One step in the story is omitted. The animals are not killed by the fire. See Zigmond-Williams version (A).

[6]It must be assumed that Coyote came along early enough to watch Crow's procedure.

[7]See note 2 above. Sadie's rendering of the Kawaiisu word as 'white shirt' was puzzling until, in 1977, Lida Girado explained that the shirt was so bright and shiny that it looked white.

me." Coyote thought he could do the same as Crow had done. Crow came over early the next day. Coyote got the fire going and waited in the center of the circle. He collected the game, but he couldn't fly out and he was burned.

22. Coyote and the Red-Headed Bird[1] (Bungling Host)

A.   CAPPANNARI (EMMA WILLIAMS: SADIE WILLIAMS)

Red-headed Bird [unidentified] had a brush house. One day Coyote visited her. She put a pot in the fire and, when the water was boiling, she put her head in it. That is why her head is red.

Soon there were suds like rice in the water, and Red-headed Bird gave them to Coyote. She said, "Eat some, and save a little for your children." Coyote put some of the suds in his net to carry them home. But when he got home, there was none left. He had eaten all of it along the way.

Coyote had invited Red-headed Bird to his house and promised to give her his star-shirt. The next day the Bird came over to visit him. He talked with her a little while. Then he said, "I don't have anything on hand to eat." He went and got a pot, put water in it, and put it on the fire. When the water boiled, he stuck his head in it. His head came off.

Red-headed Bird said to Coyote's wife, "I came to get his star-shirt." Coyote's wife answered, "He has no star-shirt--no nothing."

Red-headed Bird went home.

---

[1]This tale is one of the **series** of Bungling Host myths. As usual it involves the obtaining of food in a unique manner by the host, and Coyote's determination to try the same method. Coyote invites the host to visit him, promises him/her a "star-shirt" (which the translator often calls a "white shirt"), and goes home with food intended for his family but which he consumes completely along the way. For an explanation of the "star/white" shirt, see note 7 of the "Coyote and Crow" myth. The nature of the "suds" remains a mystery. The attitude of Coyote's wife toward him is typical.

23. Coyote and Fox

A.   ZIGMOND (EMMA WILLIAMS: ELSIE GARCIA)

Coyote was out hunting. He had his bow and arrow under his arm.
He saw Fox ahead and he stopped to watch him. Fox was shaving off his fur
with his obsidian knife. As he shaved, Fox said, "winapiži[1] ko, ko, ko, ko."
But as he shaved, his fur grew back.

Coyote was watching. When Fox stopped, Coyote walked around and
came up from the other side. Coyote asked Fox what he was doing. Fox said
he wasn't doing anything--just sitting there. But Coyote wasn't satisfied.
He saw fur lying all around. He kept asking so many questions that Fox told
him what he was doing. He showed Coyote how he shaved. Coyote watched awhile.

Coyote wanted to try it. He went home, took his obsidian knife, and
went outside. He started to shave. He shaved his whole body--head, feet,
everything. Then he said, "winapiži ko, ko, ko, ko," but the fur didn't grow
back.

The sun was going down. Coyote was getting cold. He began to
shiver. When the shade fell upon him, he followed the sunlight. He kept
going up a mountain. Then he climbed to the top of a tree on the top of the
mountain. He couldn't go any higher. The sun went down. Coyote was cold.
He died.

B.   CAPPANNARI (MARIE GIRADO: CLARA GIRADO)

[Marie did not know the beginning of this myth. She knew only how
it ended.]

Coyote had no fur. It was late in the afternoon, and to stay warm,
he kept in the sunshine. As the shade moved, he kept climbing a high hill
to be in the sunshine. Finally the sun was so low that it was shining only
on a tree on top of the hill. Coyote climbed the tree. There he froze to
death and fell from the tree.

----

[1]Winapi is an obsidian knife; winapiži is the diminutive form.

103

24. Coyote and Pitch (Tar Baby)

A.   McCOWN (RAFAEL GIRADO)

One day Coyote was walking through the woods. He was passing a
tree when he heard someone whistle and call his name. He looked around, but
couldn't see anybody. "Who knows my name?" he asked. He couldn't find anyone at all. He went along a little farther and the same thing happened.
Finally he looked up in a tree and saw *sanopi*.[1] Coyote asked, "How do you
know my name?" *Sanopi* said, "I know it." Coyote said, "Come down or I'll
kill you." *Sanopi* said, "This is my place." Coyote shot him with all his
arrows but could not kill him. Then he got mad and hit him with his bow but
that didn't kill him. Finally Coyote climbed up in the tree and hit *sanopi*
with one paw. It stuck there and he couldn't get it free. He hit him with
his other paw. It stuck too, so he kicked him with both feet. They stuck.
Then he bit *sanopi* and his teeth stuck. Coyote couldn't move. He had to
stay there and died.

B.   ZIGMOND (EMMA WILLIAMS)

Coyote was walking along with his bow and arrow under his arm. He
passed by a pinyon tree [*Pinus monophylla*]. He heard whistling: *sɨnaʔav
. . . sɨnaʔav . . . sɨnaʔavi*.[2] He stopped and looked around, but he couldn't
see anyone. He went a little farther. He heard it again and stopped. He
saw Pitch at the top of the tree. It was brown.

Coyote got angry. He said he was going to kill Pitch. He shot at
it with his bow and arrow. As the arrow hit Pitch, it said, *wižarɨ, wižarɨ*.[3]

Coyote shot all his arrows. Then he threw his bow at Pitch. Then
he climbed the tree. He rolled up his sleeves. He was going to kill Pitch.
He hit it with his fist, but the fist stuck. He hit it with the other fist.
It stuck. He kicked it with one foot. It stuck. He kicked it with the other

---

[1]*Sanapi* (or *sanapɨ*) 'pitch, gum'.

[2]Coyote's name is *sɨnaʔavi*. Apparently the whispered sounds were
produced as the wind blew over the pitch.

[3]This word appears in the John Marcus version as *kiža*. No meaning
was suggested.

105

foot. It stuck. He hit it with his head. It stuck.

Coyote couldn't get free. He died there.

C.   ZIGMOND (JOHN MARCUS)

Coyote was walking along. He heard someone calling: *kiža kiža kiža sɨnaʔavi*.[4] Coyote looked around. He heard again: *kiža kiža kiža sɨnaʔavi*.
He looked around again. He heard again: *kiža kiža kiža sɨnaʔavi*. Coyote walked slowly around a pine tree and looked up. He called out, "Say it again!"
He heard: *kiža*, etc. He kept walking around. He said, "Say it again!" He heard: *kiža*, etc. This happened three or four times. Finally he saw a black ball of pitch on the top of the pine tree. "Say it again!" he yelled. He saw Pitch open as it said: *kiža*, etc.

Coyote was very angry. "I'm going to kill you!" he said. He shot an arrow at Pitch. It stuck. "Say it again!" It said: *kiža*, etc. He shot all his arrows. They all stuck. He threw his bow. It stuck. "Say it again!" It said: *kiža*, etc.

"Now I'm going to kill you!" said Coyote. He climbed the tree.
He hit Pitch with his fist. It stuck. He hit Pitch with his other fist.
It stuck. "Say it again!" It said: *kiža*, etc. He kicked Pitch with his foot. It stuck. "Say it again!" It said: *kiža*, etc. He kicked Pitch with his other foot. "Say it again!" It said: *kiža*, etc. He hit Pitch with his head. It stuck. When Coyote's head stuck, he died.

D.   CAPPANNARI (MARIE GIRADO: CLARA GIRADO)

There was a trail over a hill. There were many pinyon trees over that hill. Coyote had his bow and arrows with him. As he was going up the hill, he was whistling a song. [Marie doesn't remember the tune.]

Someone whistled. The whistle called Coyote. Coyote wondered, "Who is that who knows my name and is calling me?" He had a bad temper. He looked up and saw that it was Pitch (*sanapi*) teasing him. Coyote became angry, and asked Pitch to come down, but Pitch wouldn't. Coyote became very angry. He said, "If you don't come down, I'll shoot you!" He had just three arrows and he shot Pitch three times. Then he threw his bow at Pitch.

Coyote was angry because he couldn't get his arrows back. He didn't seem to hurt Pitch. He was angry and hit Pitch with his hand. It stuck. He said, "I still have another hand." That stuck. He said, "I'll kick you." The foot stuck. He said, "I have another foot. I'll kick you harder." That foot stuck. He said, "I can still bite you." He did and stuck there.

_____

[4]This utterance closely resembles that recorded in the Emma Williams version except that the latter was transcribed *wižarɨ wižarɨ*.

25. Coyote and Goldfinch[1]

A.   ZIGMOND (SETIMO GIRADO: KAWAIISU TEXT EDITED BY ELSIE GARCIA)

Goldfinch made a fire in a hole. He buried himself in the fire so that only his nose was showing. He was singing like this: *amiinani k^{w}a?avayi k^{w}ašidokok amiinani k^{w}ašidokok.*[2] When he got up, he shook off the ashes, and wasn't burned.

Coyote was peeking to see what Goldfinch was doing. He said to himself, "What is that? What is that pretty little sound?" Then Coyote went over to Goldfinch and asked him, "What are you doing? Why are you doing that? What were you saying? I shall do it too."

"I am doing nothing," said Goldfinch.
"You are lying," said Coyote. "You were doing something." He kept asking questions until Goldfinch told him. "All right," said Coyote, "let me try."
"Get some wood," said Goldfinch.
"Yes, indeed," said Coyote. "I'll get wood." He made a fire and laid down on it. He wanted to sing. He tried, but he was burned up.
"Thus I kill you," said Goldfinch. "You are already nothing."

B.   CAPPANNARI (MARIE GIRADO: CLARA GIRADO)[3]

Goldfinch made a hole in the ground and put red hot coals in it. Then she[4] got in the hole and covered herself. Just her bill showed. Coyote

---

[1]Originally I called this myth "Coyote and Wild Canary" because *niwizirikiži* was described as a "little yellow bird." In 1974, Andy Greene thought it was a mockingbird; but in 1977, Lida Girado said it is a goldfinch. The latter name seems to fit the description best.

[2]The recording of the song is only approximate. In the 1930s an informant thought the first word means "I tuck under" but in the 1970s nothing of the song was recognized.

[3]Cappannari called this myth "Coyote and the Bird." Obviously Marie Girado had no suggestion as to the identity of the bird.

[4]Setimo Girado, about 1937, considered the bird a male. Ten years later his wife Marie thought of it as female.

was peeking at her all this time. She got out of the coals and shook herself. Her feathers were fluffy and pretty. She sang this song:[5]

> *Hanenena kavaya*
> *Waka kawɨzi wuzi*
> *Yu sonyiva*
> *Vayakwazi we*
> *Ohhh!*

As she sang, Goldfinch danced beautifully in the fire without getting burned.

Coyote approached and said, "Let me try it now. It is my turn to
play." He made a big fire in a hole large enough to cover him. Then he got
in the hole and cooked.

---

[5]Marie Girado knew no meaning for the words of the song, but she
thought the last line was an exclamation of pleasure.

26. Coyote and Kangaroo-rat

A.

ZIGMOND (REFUGIA WILLIAMS)

Coyote was walking in the hills. He heard Kangaroo-rat saying something like "*išbambɨ sanzun*"[1] while she cut rice-grass [*Oryzopsis hymenoides*] with her mouth.

Coyote on the other side of the hill was mocking her with his big voice. She couldn't see him. Finally he came over to where she was. He asked her what she was saying. She said, "I didn't say anything." She wouldn't tell him for a long time. He kept asking her. Then he said, "Is this what you said?" and repeated the words. She said it was. He said he was going to try it, too.

And so he tried to cut the grass with his mouth just as she did, but the straw stuck in his nose and he died.

----

[1]The words are only an approximate recording and are meaningless as they stand. Their construction suggests that they are not in the Kawaiisu language.

27. Coyote and Wasp[1]

A. ZIGMOND (EMMA WILLIAMS)

Wasp (*tavimuunikɨzɨ*) lived near the site of the power house in Isabella.[2] Every day she would take a bath in the spring pond. When she came to the pond, she would sit on a rock beside the water. She would sing a song: *činakapuri činakapuri uuhuunaakari*[3] and at the end of the song, she would say, "*cinak*," dive in, and swim to the other side.

Coyote was walking along. He heard the song. He listened to see from what direction it was coming. He went that way, hid behind a tree, and watched Wasp. Then he came up to her and asked what she was doing. She wouldn't tell him at first, but he kept asking questions, so she began to tell him. She showed him how she sang, said "*činak*," and jumped into the water. After he watched her several times, he wanted to try it.

Coyote put down his bow and arrow, got on a rock, sang in his big voice, said "*činak*" loudly, and jumped in. He didn't come up. Wasp kept watching the place where he would come up. She could see his hair under the water, but he never came up. He drowned.

B. ZIGMOND (LOUISA MARCUS)

Wasp[4] was flying up into the air from a flat rock. He sang a song:

---

[1]In the Kawaiisu Dictionary, *tavimuunikɨzɨ* is defined as a 'fly that darts rapidly back and forth'. The word is composed of two elements, *tavi* 'sun' and *muuni-* 'to buzz'. In the myth it was called a "wasp," and I have kept this designation here. The relationship between this myth and "Coyote and Ladybird" is obvious. Nevertheless it is curious that Emma Williams was the source of both of them.

[2]Like Bodfish, Isabella is on the east bank of the Kern River. The two are less than three miles apart.

[3]The words of the song were not translated, but "wasp" says *činak* as she dives into the water.

[4]The Kawaiisu word used here is the same as that employed in Emma Williams' "Wasp" myth. This is the only tale recorded from Louisa Marcus,

ulali tapičik^w e?ani ta...o...sak^w ik,[5] flew into the air, and returned to the rock. Coyote saw him from behind the brush.

Coyote came over to Wasp. "What are you doing?" he asked. "I am not doing anything," said Wasp. "You're lying," said Coyote. "You were doing something."

Coyote put his rabbitskin blanket around Wasp. "When you go up in the air, you will look pretty," said Coyote. Wasp flew up and came down. Coyote said, "It's pretty. It's pretty. Try it again." Wasp went up a second time. He flew away and never came back. Coyote was watching him. He yelled at him and told him to bring down the blanket. Wasp kept going straight on and never came back.

Coyote was cold. He kept following the sun, trying to keep warm. He reached the top of the mountain. The sun went down. Coyote was very cold. He died.

---

though her husband John was one of my chief informants. While the characters are the same as those in the other version, the story is different.

[5]No meaning of the song was given. The presence of *l*'s in the first word may indicate that the language is not Kawaiisu. However, the second word has *tapiči*- which means 'to tie' in Kawaiisu.

28. Coyote and Ladybird[1]

A.   CAPPANNARI (EMMA WILLIAMS: SADIE WILLIAMS)

Across the river from the Bodfish Post Office, there is a spring. Ladybird was diving into it. She had long pretty hair. Before diving, she sat on a little rock and sang, *činakapuri činakapuri hu hu nakari*.[2]

Coyote heard the song, and he sneaked up and watched her from behind a bush. Then he came over and asked her what she was doing. Ladybird said, "Nothing. I'm just sitting here." She sang again, dove into the water, and then got back on the rock.

Coyote said, "Let me try that." He sang, too. Then he dove into the water. He never came up. His hair floated on the surface.

---

[1]Though Cappannari assumed that "ladybird" is an unidentified bird with the Kawaiisu name *činakapuri*, more likely it is the insect variously called "ladybird," "ladybug," "ladybeetle," "ladyfly." This suggestion is supported by the fact that the story is the same as that involving "wasp" (q.v.) who sings the same song but whose Kawaiisu name is *tavimuunikɨzɨ*. It is possible that Cappannari did not ask Emma and Sadie what kind of a "bird" ladybird is.

[2]These words are not translated. However, "wasp" says "*činak*" as she dives into the water. In the Zigmond version of "Coyote and Wasp," *hu hu nakari* is recorded *uuhuunaakari*.

29. Coyote and the Leaves

A.   ZIGMOND (EMMA WILLIAMS)

Coyote was going visiting. He was going up a trail that passed by
a cottonweed tree [*Populus fremontii*]. The leaves of the tree whistled and
said, "*sɨnaʔav...sɨnaʔav...sɨnaʔavi...*" Coyote stopped and asked, "How do
they know my name is *sɨnaʔavi*?" He went a little farther. He heard it again.
He stopped and looked up. There were just a few leaves on the cottonwood
tree. When the wind went through them, it made them whistle.

Coyote heard the song of the leaves: *mɨvaʔeena kʷariʔina kʷiterivi
kʷiterivi put put put.*[1] Coyote liked it. He was going to try to sing. He
put down his bow and arrow. The wind kept the leaves singing. Coyote sang
in his loud voice. He had to "catch his breath," but he grew tired. He ran
out of breath and died.

---

[1]The recording is only approximate. No translation was volunteered.
In such cases the narrator often remarked that she did not know the meaning.

30. Coyote and Worm

A.   ZIGMOND (SETIMO GIRADO)

Coyote was coming down the trail. He heard someone calling his name: *sɨnaʔavi, sɨnaʔavi*. He [Coyote?] whistled. "Who knows my name?" he asked. He looked all around. He couldn't see anyone. Then he found *čičiyogozi*[1] [earthworm or angleworm] in the grass.

Coyote wanted to use Worm for a belt because he was shiny. He tried him on as a belt, but he didn't like it. He put him on his wrist as a bracelet, but he didn't like it. He tried him around his neck, and he liked it there.

He walked away from there like that. Worm kept getting tighter around his neck. Coyote tried to loosen him up, but he got tighter than ever. Worm dug into Coyote's neck. Coyote fell down and choked to death.

B.   CAPPANNARI (MARIE GIRADO: CLARA GIRADO)

Coyote often went to Sand Canyon. One day he was walking in that direction whistling, when he heard someone else whistle. He stopped and said, "I wonder who that could be calling my name." He could see no one. When he looked under a large bush there was a large black worm with a washboard-like waist. He tried it on as a bracelet and also as a belt. He thought, "Maybe it would make a nice necklace. That's more like it."

He started up the road again whistling. As he walked along, it began to feel a little snug. He loosened it, but soon it got even tighter. He said, "What's wrong with this? It seems to be getting tighter." He loosened it once more and then it began to choke him. He begged it to stop but it kept getting tighter and finally choked him.

----

[1]Setimo Girado described the *čičiyogozi* as a large brown worm with a shell-like back. Clara Girado pictured it as a large black worm.

31. Coyote, Hummingbird, and Rattlesnake

A.   McCOWN (RAFAEL GIRADO)

There was a deep gorge between two high mountains. At the bottom of the gorge was Rattlesnake. He had many teeth--more than he has now. Up in the air was Hummingbird. He would dive down at Rattlesnake, and as Rattlesnake struck at him, Hummingbird would pull out one of his teeth.

Coyote came by and heard the fight. He sneaked up, hid behind a bush, and watched what was going on. He thought, "I can do that too," so he came out in the open, called to Hummingbird, and said to him, "Let me try." Hummingbird replied, "You are too slow. You will get killed." Coyote said, "No, I will do it anyway."

So Coyote went up to the top of one of the high mountains, and ran down as fast as he could. But he was too slow. Rattlesnake struck him and hit him. Coyote was killed, and he turned into a rock.

Hummingbird had tried to pull all of Rattlesnake's teeth out and make him harmless, but Coyote spoiled it all. Rattlesnake has four teeth now.

The name of the place where the fight took place is *togoinapina*.[1]

----

[1]The first element of this word would seem to be derived from *togowa* 'rattlesnake'.

32. Coyote and Louse[1]

A.

CAPPANNARI (MARIE GIRADO: CLARA GIRADO)

Coyote lived in a brush house in the canyon. He was lying on his back resting. He did this every day.

A beautiful woman was coming up the canyon. She was white and had large breasts. Except for a breechclout, she was naked. Coyote watched her and was just about crazy with lust. "My, what a beautiful woman!" he thought. She walked past his place. As she passed, she jiggled her breasts and sang: *carali topa topa, carali topa topa.*[2]

Coyote ran from his house. He knew the canyon well and in which direction she was headed, so he rushed ahead of her. Then he built a house along the way, and made it look as if he had always lived there. Even the ashes in the fireplace looked old. He saw the woman coming, and watched her. Again she passed him by. Again he rushed ahead and prepared another "old" house. Again he watched. This time, as she passed by, he chased her, caught and held her. He told her what he was going to do with her. He couldn't wait; he wanted to have intercourse right then. Just as he was about to begin, she disappeared. He found her on his penis in the form of a little white bug.[3] He gave an exclamation of disgust: *eu nɨwɨ* [what a person!]. He took the bug off and threw it away.

That meant that there were going to be white people.

---

[1]Cappannari's title for this tale is "First White Woman" which would seem to miss the point. He probably derived this title from the final sentence of the story which may reflect Clara Girado's comment. The similarity of the tale to the Chemehuevi myth recorded by Laird (1976:149f.) is noted in the Introduction.

[2]No translation was suggested.

[3]Kawaiisu *poʔovi* means 'body louse'; Cappannari may have been unaware of this.

33. Coyote and Bat[1]

A.
ZIGMOND (SETIMO GIRADO)

    All the people had houses. Coyote made a fire in his winter-house.[2]
A live coal went up out of the smoke-hole at the top of his house. It went
high. Bat came down to get the coal. He put it under his wing. He went home
and made a fire with it. Coyote asked him, "Where did you get that fire?"
Bat said, "I got it in the air."

    Everyone went hunting. Coyote and Bat went, too. Everyone killed
deer except Coyote and Bat. Bat went to the water to get some ice. He said,
"*para?asi yuhuviči*" ['ice-fat'].[3] He was eating the ice by the fire. The
ice was melting. Bat didn't want anyone to see it. He called the ice "fat."
He was ashamed because he hadn't killed anything. He wanted people to think
that he was eating the grease of an animal. Coyote saw that it was ice. He
said, "Shame on you! You got that down by the water."

B.
CAPPANNARI (?)

    Bat[4] was a young man. He had lots of women around him. They lived
together. But he was not a good hunter. Every morning he went out and
claimed he killed a deer, but he wouldn't eat it facing the women. He always ate facing the wall. He said that it was a very fat deer which he had
cooked, and that was fat running down his elbow. It was really a melting
icicle, running down his elbow.

------

[1]One of the several adventures related in the Chemehuevi myth
"How Yucca Date Worm Girls Went to Look for a Husband" is an episode which
closely parallels this tale (Laird 1976:163-4). It is discussed in the Introduction.

[2]The *tomokahni* 'winter-house' was the regular shelter of the
Kawaiisu, though in mild weather they might spend much of their time in the
tavikahni 'sun-house' or *havakahni* 'shade-house'.

[3]'Ice' (*para?asipɨ* is literally 'frozen water'; *yuhuvɨ* [or *yɨhuvɨ*]
is 'fat' or 'grease'--*yuhuviči* is a diminutive form).

[4]Cappannari calls this myth "Bat" since Coyote plays no part in it.
The name of the narrator is omitted.

34. Coyote and Wildcat

A.

ZIGMOND (EMMA WILLIAMS)

Wildcat had the tail feather of Eagle on his arrow. Coyote had the tail feather of Squirrel Hawk on his arrow. Wildcat and Coyote were neighbors; their houses were close together. When they went out hunting, Wildcat would always get something. Coyote wouldn't; he would miss every time. Coyote would follow Wildcat around. Whenever Wildcat shot at a jackrabbit, he would say "*kamɨrui*"[1] and would kill the rabbit. Coyote said Wildcat was killing all the rabbits and there weren't any where he was. He wanted to trade arrows, and so they traded. Then when they went out hunting, Coyote killed the rabbits and Wildcat didn't kill one.

Wildcat got thin and weak, but he went out hunting anyway. He got on a hill and said, "I wish Coyote would hit a jackrabbit so that it would run to me and bring my arrow back." Just then he heard a noise and saw a rabbit with his arrow. Coyote was hunting all over for the arrow. Wildcat got his own arrow back, and threw Coyote's arrow away.

B.

ZIGMOND (SETIMO GIRADO)

Coyote came down a sandy place. He was walking and singing: *wailaskimat ʔuʔuwayesani*[2] [repeated]. He met Wildcat and they went hunting jackrabbits. Wildcat killed many rabbits; Coyote killed none. Coyote said, "My arrow is no good. Yours is good. I can't kill anything with mine." And so they traded arrows.

Next morning they went hunting again. Coyote killed many rabbits; Wildcat killed nothing. Wildcat said, "I don't like your arrow."

They were sitting in the *tavikahni*.[3] Coyote scratched Wildcat's face. Coyote said, "I have long claws." Wildcat said, "Let me try." He scratched Coyote's face so that the blood ran. Coyote yelled.

---

[1]*Kamɨ* means 'jackrabbit'.

[2]Setimo said the words mean 'running-trotting'. It is likely that they are from another language.

[3]'Sunhouse'--usually a brush enclosure.

Wildcat wanted his arrow back. Coyote gave it back.

Wildcat went where there were many people. He killed a cottontail on his way. He came to an old man[4] who was sleeping by a fire. Wildcat roasted the cottontail in the hot coals. The man woke up. He smelled something good to eat. He said, "What are you roasting?" Wildcat said, "Do you want some of it?" He gave the man a little piece. He liked it and wanted more. He said, "Many people are going to come here tonight." He hid Wildcat.

The "people" were jackrabbits. They played the stick-guessing game.[5] Wildcat was watching from the outside. When daylight came, the rabbits were leaving the house. Wildcat had a long stick and with it he killed every one of them. The old man helped him. They roasted some.

Wildcat said, "I'm going home. I won't come back." He went home.[6]

Wildcats kill jackrabbits and cottontails to this day.

---

[4]The name of the "old man" was *kokopakazi*, said to be a bird that looks like a robin.

[5]The stick-guessing game (*sɨrɨgɨ-*) involves the holding of a stick in one hand with both hands folded. The opponent must guess the hand in which the stick is held.

[6]It will be noted that Setimo Girado's version of this myth has two parts. Coyote figures in the first part but not in the second. The second part is similar to Refugia Williams' "Wildcat and 'Man'." Refugia did not identify the "man," but here Setimo identifies him as *kokopakazi*, a robin-like bird.

35. Coyote and the Weather

A.   ZIGMOND (EMMA WILLIAMS: ELSIE GARCIA)

Coyote lived in Kelso Valley in a rock house. It was very hot.
There was no breeze in the house. He took a stick and poked holes in the
roof. You can still see the house with the holes.

Coyote was very smart. He thought of a way of getting a breeze.
He went to the top of Piute Mountain with his flute. There was a flat rock
on which he lay and played his flute. As he played, the fog came up. As
soon as it came near him, he ran to his house. But the fog would not follow
him. It went back to Bakersfield.[1] He returned to the rock the next day and
played again. As he played, he would get up to see if the fog was coming.
It came. He ran to his house, but the fog went back to Bakersfield.

On the third day he decided not to run home but to stay until the
fog came to him. He played his flute and kept on playing. It started to rain.
Then it snowed. He was about to head for home while it was snowing, but he
couldn't make it. He was snowed in. You can still see the place on the rock
where he lay. His flute grew into an elderberry tree[2] near the rock. You
can still see his hair which is the moss (*paazimoʔora*) on the white pine tree.

Coyote died there.

B.   ZIGMOND (SETIMO GIRADO)

Coyote lived in Kelso Valley where he had a house of rock with holes
in it. It is still there. He lived there with his wife and children.

Coyote went up to a flat rock on a mountain called *paazimoʔora*.
He lay down on the rock, shut his eyes, and played on his flute. He wanted
to bring rain. A fog came up, but when he opened his eyes, the fog went
back [from where it came]. He tried a second time. The same thing happened.

---

[1] If the fog went from Bakersfield (in the San Joaquin Valley) to
Piute Mountain and thence to Kelso Valley, it would be moving in a fairly
straight line eastward.

[2] Flutes were made of elderberry wood (*Sambucus* sp.).

He tried it a third time. As he played his flute, his scrotum made a black mark on the rock[3] which can still be seen.

The third time he saw snow coming. He ran very fast. You can still see his tracks in the rock. The snow caught up with him and piled high. Coyote was cold. He turned to rock. He can still be seen with his nose pointed upward.

Coyote's hair is the moss called *paazimo?ora* which grows on trees.[4] If you put it in water, fog and cold will come.

C.   CAPPANNARI (EMMA WILLIAMS: SADIE WILLIAMS)

In the summer, Coyote lived in a cave in Kelso Valley. It was too hot inside so he made holes in it with his stick.

Coyote played music on his elderberry flute. Later in the year he walked over to this side of the mountains. He played his flute and that made the fog come up the canyon toward him. He ran back to his house, going on the side of the mountains where there was no fog. Then he returned to the canyon and played his flute. Again the fog came. He thought, "I'll wait until it gets here and then go home."[5] When the fog came, it snowed. He tried to get home, but the snow was too high. He sat down on a big rock and died there. He turned to rock and is still there.

Elderberry trees grew from his flute. The fir trees have moss which is really Coyote's hair (*pazimora*). You can see his tracks on that rock. They are long, like a baby track.

D.   CAPPANNARI (MARIE GIRADO: CLARA GIRADO)

Coyote made a flute out of elderberry wood. He removed the pith and it was hollow.[6] Coyote went up a mountain this side of Piute. He was lying on a rock, playing his flute. As he started playing, he saw clouds coming in his direction. He thought it was going to snow and became frightened. He stopped playing and the clouds went away. He started again and the same thing happened. Finally he started enjoying his music so much that he paid no attention to the clouds. It began to snow. He started to run but it was too late. He reached a rock and couldn't go any farther. He died there.

You can see that rock now. It is shaped like a man. The imprint of his body—feet, testicles, etc.—is on the rock. That flute became an

---

[3]Literally translated: 'His testicles turned the rock black'.

[4]The moss, *Ramalina menziesii*, and the mountain had the same name.

[5]This version, differing from that which Emma Williams told Zigmond ten years earlier, does not indicate that Coyote was seeking to have cooler weather follow him to his house.

[6]This is the way Kawaiisu flutes were made, but no mention is made here of the single row of holes for the fingers.

elderberry tree. His hair hangs on the trees there. It is called *pazimora*. If you put *pazimora* in water, sleet and freezing weather will come. If you pick it now [in the summer], it might rain.[7] The name of the mountain where Coyote died is *pazimora*.

E.   McCOWN (NO INFORMANT NAMED)[8]

Coyote lay on a big rock and called rain from over Bakersfield. There are marks on the rock of Coyote's testicles and feet. Coyote called several times. A big wind and snow came. It blew Coyote through the pass.[9] His fur stuck to the oak and pine trees (a form of Spanish moss or lichen).[10] It blew him into Kelso Valley. If the "fur" is put into water bottles,[11] it brings rain. But one has to know how to do this.

F.   McCOWN (SANTOS PHILLIPS)

Coyote played a flute to call rain from over Bakersfield. [He][12] played a long time on his flute and got very sleepy. Finally the rain came.

G.   McCOWN (SANTOS PHILLIPS)

Coyote wanted to make rain. [He] smoked a long pipe. [He] went to sleep near *pazimora* and it rained and snowed. Coyote died. Pine trees grew up near there with green and black hair on them. This is Coyote fur. If this is put in water bottles, it makes rain, snow, and cold weather.

---

[7]Marie Girado added that she "had some, but was afraid to bring it out--it might cause rain and ruin her garden." More information on this subject is to be found in my paper on *The Supernatural World of the Kawaiisu* (Zigmond 1977).

[8]McCown captions this paragraph "The Outline or base of a Coyote-rain tale."

[9]The pass is not identified.

[10]This is a tree moss, *Ramalina menziesii*.

[11]Putting moss in water-bottles would be a problem in view of their restricted necks. The usual statement is that the moss is put in water.

[12]I have added "he" to round out the sentence.

36. Coyote and Turtle

A.

ZIGMOND (SETIMO GIRADO)

Coyote and Turtle went hunting. Both of them had children. Turtle killed a deer; Coyote killed nothing. Coyote said, "Let's try jumping over the deer. Whoever jumps over it will have it." Coyote told Turtle to jump, but Turtle landed on the deer's stomach. Coyote said, "Let me try." He jumped over the deer. Coyote claimed the deer and took it home.

Coyote and his children ate up the deer. They gave nothing to Turtle or his children. Turtle's children were starving. Turtle was angry. He made the sun so hot that the water boiled in the lake. Coyote and his children were hot so they jumped into the lake. After they jumped into the boiling water, their bones kept coming up. They all died.

B.

CAPPANNARI (MARIE GIRADO: CLARA GIRADO)

One morning Coyote and Turtle went hunting together. Turtle killed a large deer; Coyote didn't get anything (he doesn't really know how to hunt deer). While they were butchering the deer, Coyote said, "Whoever can jump farthest over the deer should have it all." Coyote knew Turtle couldn't jump. Turtle didn't want to do it, but he agreed. Coyote jumped 'way over the deer. Then Turtle tried and landed right on the deer's stomach. So Coyote won the deer. Each of them had large families. Coyote gave Turtle the paunch. This made Turtle very angry. He took the paunch home with him, but instead of cleaning the paunch, he put the whole thing in the fire to cook it. It exploded and burst all over his family. That made Turtle even angrier. He sang:[1]

> kɨsɨrɨɨ
> kɨsɨrɨɨ
> yatabe okatse
> yatapɨmo katse

It got so hot that Coyote and his family couldn't stand it. The water in the stream was boiling. Coyote and the family jumped into the water.

---

[1]Clara Girado said the words mean: "He wanted the ground to get so hot that even greasewood would smell." The words 'steam' (kosowaagi-) and 'greasewood' (yatabɨ) are apparently in the song if one corrects the faulty recording. It may be, therefore, that Clara's rough translation conveys the sense.

They cooked so fast that their bones boiled to the surface.

After Turtle got rid of Coyote and his family, he said, "*mani kai ivana.*"[2]

---

[2]Again a faulty recording apparently obscures the meaning.

37. Coyote and Badger

A.   ZIGMOND (EMMA WILLIAMS: ELSIE GARCIA)

There were many holes in which the squirrels lived. Badger would go there every morning and lay down. He had a long stick which he put beside him. He would lie there for awhile and the little squirrels would come out of the holes. They thought he was asleep or dead, and he pretended ·as if he were. They would look at his paws, into his eyes, into his ears, his nose, his mouth. When they came to the white streak on Badger's head and nose, they thought it was very pretty and asked what it was. They turned him over and felt him all around. But Badger gave no sign of life.

Then the middle-sized squirrels would come out and the same thing happened. Badger didn't stir. Finally the large squirrels would come out and do the same thing. But as soon as a number of the large squirrels were around him, he would get up quickly and kill them with his stick.

He did this every morning.

One day Coyote came along and found Badger like dead. He waited and watched to see what would happen. Coyote asked Badger how he caught the squirrels. Badger said he didn't do anything, but Coyote kept asking him until he told.

Coyote went home and tried to sleep, but he was so eager to catch the squirrels that he kept getting up. He arose early in the morning and went where there were many holes. He lay down with a stick. The little squirrels came out of the holes. They looked into his eyes, his ears, his nose, his feet. They turned him over. Pretty soon they came to his ribs. He began to laugh. The squirrels ran away. He caught a few of the little ones and ate them right away without taking them home.

38. Coyote and Lady Bear

A.

CAPPANNARI (MARIE GIRADO)

One day Lady Bear was taking a nap. It was warm and she was lying in the sun. While she was sleeping, Coyote came along and had intercourse with her. Just when he finished, she awakened. She was so angry with him that she wanted to kill him. Coyote fled to the hills and Bear ran after him. By the time she got to the top of one hill, Coyote was already on another. So they went from one hill to the next. Lady Bear didn't catch him.

39. Coyote and the Grinding Slab

A.   CAPPANNARI (MARIE GIRADO)

One day Coyote went to get some willow branches to make a shade house. He was among the willows breaking off pieces, but he saw a couple of old women grinding *ku?u* seed [*Mentzelia* species][1] nearby. The women asked for help. They wanted Coyote to grind the seed. He started to grind it on a grinding slab, but the slab began to rise in the air. He tried to hold it down but he couldn't. The old women chuckled; they must have been witches. Every time Coyote tried to hold down the grinding slab, it would lift him into the air and he would drop it. He said, "*pitana siwa?a kuuwaa.*"[2] It kept rising and falling. It landed on Coyote's head.

---

[1]Several *Mentzelia* species yield edible seeds. The plants are commonly called 'stickseed' or 'blazing star'.

[2]The Kawaiisu words must be regarded as only approximate. *Pitani-* is a root meaning 'to hurry'. A pun may be involved in the word *ku?u*. It refers both to the *Mentzelia* plant and also means 'to catch'. Hence the interpreter translated the three Kawaiisu words: "Hurry up and catch it."

40. Coyote and the Basket[1]

A.   ZIGMOND (MARTINA COLLINS)[2]

Coyote was in South Fork[3] and was carrying a basket with many children in it. He was going up to Inyo County.[4] He grew tired, took the basket off his back, and set it on the ground. The children came out of the basket and ran away. They scattered all over. Coyote tried to catch them, but he couldn't catch any. He cried.

He had wanted to take them to Mono Lake.[5]

---

[1]This brief story is reminiscent of the episode included by Laird (1976:151) in the Chemehuevi myth "How People Were Made." Coyote "opened the basket, and immediately people began pouring out and scattering in all directions, over the whole face of the earth." In a personal communication (1937), Gayton noted the similarity of the Kawaiisu story to the "episode from the Basin tale of the beginning of tribes."

[2]Martina Collins was an old woman when I met her in 1936. I have the impression that the few myths I obtained from her could have been considerably lengthened with more adequate means of communication.

[3]The South Fork of the Kern River was the main dwelling area of the Tübatulabal, just north of the Kawaiisu region.

[4]Inyo County is north of Kern County where both the Kawaiisu and the Tübatulabal live.

[5]Mono Lake is in Mono County, north of Inyo County.

41. The Race from Victorville to Koso Hot Springs[1]

A.   ZIGMOND (EMMA WILLIAMS: ELSIE GARCIA)[2]

Coyote was the chief of the animals.

All the birds, animals, frogs, lizards, snakes came from Koso
Springs to Victorville to eat the sugar found in carizzo grass, 'cane'
[*pagabɨ*, *Phragmites australis*]. Before they started, they dug a big hole,
built a fire in it, and boiled water. They left Robin behind to tend the
boiling of the water. He has a red breast because of the heat of the fire
and the boiling water.

The animals agreed to race back from Victorville to Koso. Those
who got back last were to be thrown in the boiling water. That was Coyote's
idea. The others didn't like it, but Coyote knew that he could run fast.

Everyone went and ate sugar all day long. By the afternoon Coyote
was getting tired and full. He whistled and asked, "Are you ready yet [to
start back]?" He could hear the answer "No," and he could hear the animals.
So he ate some more. Then he asked again and received the same answer. But
the other animals had really gone. They wanted to get a head start on Coyote.
It was the *inɨpi* who had answered and the noise was the wind.

At length Coyote grew suspicious and looked around. He found that
everyone had gone. He started to run, and ran very fast. Soon he caught up
with the slowest animals. He came up to Bull Frog, urinated[3] on him, and went
on. Bull Frog made a big jump, but Coyote passed him again. Coyote overtook
all of them, urinating on them as he passed, and calling out, "You can't beat

---

[1]Comment by Gayton (personal communication 1937): "'Race of animals' is Wobonuch Western Mono (Gayton, aberrant form); Tübatulabal (C. F.
and E. W. Voegelin, ms.); Owens Valley Paiute (Steward, *Myths of the Owens
Valley Paiute*, 1936:412, 416, 436)."

[2]This version incorporates a few emendations suggested by Sam Willie
and John Marcus. Emma Williams approved the changes.

[3]Emma Williams, following her usual practice of not giving me the
"vulgar facts," substituted the word "spit." However, it is clear that Coyote
was urinating on his competitors.

141

me!" He passed them one by one. He caught up with Grizzly Bear and Brown Bear. He urinated on them and called out, "You can't beat me!" Sun was in the race and Coyote passed him, too.

Coyote was among the first to reach Koso and so were the Lizard Brothers. The Bears, Sun, and other slow animals were to be thrown in the boiling water. The others objected to Coyote's throwing Sun into the water. They said, "Everything will be dark." But Coyote said, "He would have thrown me in if he had beaten me." Sun went in and so did the others, but Bear growled. He didn't want to go in. Coyote said, "If you had beaten me, I would have gone in willingly." And so Bear went in. When they put Sun in, it became dark and stayed dark for a year. The water of the Spring was hot. It boils even now, and it makes a noise from the growling of the Bear.

It was so dark that the animals couldn't see to eat anything, so they stayed in the house all summer and all winter. In the spring, the grass was green. The two Lizard Brothers had their bed near the door. They would sneak out, chew grass, and come back in. When Coyote heard them chewing, he asked what they were eating. They said they were not eating anything. But the Brothers whispered to each other that it was spring, and Coyote heard them.

All the animals got together in the dark house to estimate how many months there would be in a winter. Each took his turn at expressing his idea. Coyote said, "As many months as there are hairs on a mouse and down on the four feathers of the owl." But the others didn't like that—it was too long. They all had their guesses. The Lizard Brothers heard the arguing. They talked the South Fork language:[4] "igiš igiš pai mɨgayil [three months in winter]." Everybody agreed to this except Coyote. He didn't like it. He got mad and wanted to kill the Lizard Brothers. They ran into a little hole. Coyote poured hot ashes into the hole so that the Brothers couldn't get out. But the ashes didn't stay hot. The Brothers waited and after the ashes cooled they came out.

The animals wondered how they could get Sun to come up again. Each one had his own idea. Coyote wanted Owl and Mallard to "crow." They crowed. Dawn could be seen, but Coyote didn't want these two to get all the credit for getting Sun up. He said, "Let me crow." As soon as he crowed, Sun went down. The other animals were angry. Everyone wanted Owl and Mallard to crow, but as soon as they did, Coyote would start again. The others warned Coyote not to crow. Finally Owl and Mallard got Sun up. The animals saw that everything was green outside. There were berries. They started to eat.

Coyote went out to eat. He got a handful of huʔupi berries [box thorn, Lycium andersonii]. He put them in his mouth and said, "paaraʔwe."[5] As soon as he said that, a rattlesnake bit him and he died of the bite.

---

[4]This is Tübatulabal spoken along the South Fork of the Kern River. The recording of the words is only approximate.

[5]This is apparently a bird identified as a whippoorwill, though I have recorded its name as paarag^wiži. No reason is given for Coyote's utterance, but there is a close parallel to be found in a Chemehuevi myth. See Introduction.

They used to live up at Koso[7] near Inyokern. They all went to Los Angeles[8] where the race would start. Koso was the end of the race. They had a fire going at Koso and the losers were to be thrown into the fire.

There were many people in the race: Coyote, Frog, Sun, spiders, little bugs, etc. Frog leaped over many hills each time he jumped. Coyote didn't like the way Frog was going. Every time Frog landed, Coyote urinated on him. Then Frog would wait until the others caught up with him.

Coyote arrived there first. When the others got to Koso, Coyote threw them into the fire. Sun said to Coyote, "I would not have thrown you in the fire if I had won the race." Coyote replied, "Yes, you would have," and threw Sun in the fire. The world began to get dark.

There were some people who had not joined in the race. The two Lizard Brothers had not been in the race, and they went into a brush house. Duck went into the house. They wouldn't let Coyote in because they were mad at him. Coyote was "hollering around and yelling." Soon he was so tired that he was crawling around on his knees. "Let me in," he said. "Where are you people? Where is the house? Who will think of things if you don't let me in?" The Lizard Brothers said, "Let's let him in, then." Coyote lay down in the house to rest.

The Lizard Brothers sneaked out to get something to eat. They were eating tickseed leaves.[9] They brought the food into the house. Coyote could hear them eating. "Give me some or I'll starve," he said. "Who will think of things if I die?" They fed him. It stayed dark for a year.

Coyote said, "Let me think. Where have you been getting this food?" "Near here," they said. They tried to think of a way to get Sun back. Coyote told Duck to quack loudly three times. Duck did, and Sun started to rise. They could see daybreak now. Coyote said, "You must let me holler, too. Why should you do all the hollering?" He started howling and it became dark. Sun was his enemy. They all told Coyote to keep quiet from then on. Duck quacked three times and Sun came all the way up.

When Sun came out, they all went and looked at the tickseed plant. Coyote helped himself. Then he urinated all over the plant and ruined it.

---

[6]Cappannari captions this version "Extinction of Sun." He neglects to indicate the narrator, but if his other version was told to him by Emma Williams, Marie Girado must be the author of this one.

[7]Cappannari adds parenthetically: "(Hot Springs)." Koso is about thirty miles from Inyokern.

[8]Los Angeles is not mentioned in the other versions.

[9]The leaves of the tickseed plant, *tɨhɨvidɨbɨ*, *Coreopsis bigelovii*, are eaten raw in the spring.

After that they decided what they were going to be.[10] Coyote said,
"I'm going to be coyote. When I die, I'll be in the canyon. I'll eat people."
Eagle decided to be eagle; Lizard, lizard. Duck said, "I'll be a duck and
live in the water." Coyote said, "I'll live in the mountains. People must
die or the world will be crowded."

C.   CAPPANNARI[11]

Coyote, Snake, Turtle, Lizard, and Sun lived in Koso. Every day
they went across the desert to Victorville[12] and ate *parabiyeve* (sugar).[13]
Each evening they returned to Koso.

One day some birds made a big fire at Koso. The mud is still boiling there.[14] Robin got too near the fire and his breast turned red. Another
bird, *yunara*,[15] got too near the fire and his eyes turned red.

Once, when they made their usual trip to the desert, they agreed to
race back to Koso. The last one[16] to get there would be thrown into the fire.
Coyote was busy eating sugar and didn't know that the others had already left.
He whistled, and they whistled back. But when he looked in the direction
from which the whistle came, he saw that no one was there. Maybe it was a
"devil" (*unupi*) who whistled.[17] Coyote looked in the distance and saw some
dust rising in the air. He started running as fast as he could. He passed
Turtle, Snake, and Lizard. Each time he passed anyone, he urinated on him.
Coyote was the first to arrive at Koso. Bear arrived next and Coyote caught
him and threw him into the fire. Next he burned Turtle, Snake, and Lizard.
Then he threw Sun into the fire. It became dark.

Everyone went into a brush house. There was a hot stove[18] in the
middle of the house and they sat around it talking. They had nothing to eat.
They discussed how many months there should be in the year. Coyote counted

---

[10]This discussion is sometimes found in another context and at
greater length. See "The Discussion of the Animals."

[11]Cappannari calls this myth "Sun Destruction." He does not identify
his informant, but it must have been either Emma Williams or Marie Girado--
probably the former.

[12]As the crow flies, the distance between Koso and Victorville is
over a hundred miles. The other versions do not suggest that the trip was
made every day.

[13]*Pagabihavi* combines two words: *pagabɨ*, carizzo grass (*Phragmites
australis*), and *pihavi*, sugar.

[14]As Cappannari notes, this is Koso Hot Springs.

[15]The bird is unidentified.

[16]More logically this should read "the last ones."

[17]The *ɨnɨpi* plays a similar role in other myths.

[18]The "stove" is a modern touch. Aboriginally a fire would have been
built in the center of the house.

the hairs in Mouse's fur and two Owl feathers and said there should be many months in each season.

Owl and Mallard wanted Sun to rise, and they went outside. Mallard quacked, Owl hooted, and daylight came. Coyote went outside and hollered, and it became dark again. Owl hooted, Mallard quacked, and Sun rose again. Coyote howled and again it became dark. Everyone was angry with Coyote. Maybe they would have to stay in the brush house all winter.

The two Lizard Brothers went outside, found some grass, and started eating. Coyote heard them and asked them what they were eating. They replied that they were not eating anything. The Lizard Brothers discussed how many months there should be in each season. They talked the Tübatulabal language and decided each season should have three months. The other people agreed, but Coyote became very angry. The Lizards hid in a hole. Coyote threw hot ashes into the hole. The Lizards drew some sinews out of their bodies and threw them on the ashes. The sinews sizzled loudly and Coyote believed he had killed the Brothers. Then they came out of the hole and continued eating grass.

After that the sun rose. It was spring. Everything was green and the berries were ripe. Coyote ate some of those berries.[19] While he was eating them a Rattlesnake bit him, and he died.

---

[19]Cappannari adds parenthetically: "(like those that grow in Mohave)." They would probably have been the berries of the box thorn, *Lycium andersonii*.

42. The Race Between Frog, Coyote and the Sun[1]

A.   McCOWN (SANTOS PHILLIPS)[2]

      It started from a lake below Tehachapi.[3] Frog was going to win sun.[4] Coyote catch up and win sun--sun go in desert--Hot Springs. Frog win. Coyote put Sun in lake--all dark like winter--nothing for one year. *Kwoca*-- the name of the hot springs. *Mouta*--a place way up in desert.[5] *Tarawipo'o*-- hot springs or hot water.[6] Sun comes out in the spring--everyone hollers. Duck from South Fork[7] hollered three times--sun comes up a little bit each time and runs again. Spring comes and everything is green. The hot spring was made by the sun going into the earth. Coyote and Frog race the sun. Coyote and Frog win so the sun goes in the ground. *Tcokopic*[8] was the frog's name that won from the Sun. Not the little frog, *wagata*. The start of the race was at the lake near Monolith.[9] The people were discussing the race and who was going to win. When the sun came out it was March. Coyote runs and is nearly gone out. Frog knew he was going to win all the time. Eagle, Bear, Mountain Lion were chiefs. Said: Let 'em go, don't put them in the fire. When the Sun came out it was in the East. [North and South before??] Moon was partner of the Sun. Would not come out during the long night. Mad and

------

[1]This is the title given to this myth by McCown. However, as will be seen, the basic elements are those to be found in the several versions of "The Race from Victorville to Koso Hot Springs."

[2]McCown recorded the myth in telegraphic fashion, and I have not attempted to revise it. As it stands, it lacks clarity and consistency.

[3]There is a small lake not far from Tehachapi, but it does not figure in the other versions of the "race."

[4]The meaning of "to win sun" is not clear. Perhaps it indicates that sun was to be defeated in the race.

[5]*Mu?ota* is the Kawaiisu name for Koso Hot Springs. I do not recognize *kwoca*; it may refer to "Koso."

[6]*Taru?i(dɨ)* is 'hot'; *po?o* is 'water' or 'spring'.

[7]'South Fork' refers to the South Fork of the Kern River.

[8]*Cokopu?iši* is 'bull frog'.

[9]Monolith and Tehachapi are about four miles apart. The reference is probably to the same lake as above.

would not come out. Sun was moon's uncle--*cinena*--mother's brother.[10]

B.   McCOWN (CHARLEY HASLEM)

     The Sun is a big man. In the race between Sun and Frog, the
latter had a "feather" and all the other racers lost except Frog. *Waghata*,
the frog, was red and big. There was a whistle made of a doble[11] leaf and
spittle. The Sun went into the ground because he lost the race.

     Coyote was killed by Rattlesnake.

---

    [10]*Sina=* is 'mother's younger brother'.

    [11]Double (?).

148

43. The Race Between Coot and Falcon

A.   McCOWN (JOHN NICHOLS)

Near the beginning of the Kern River in the mountains there is a rock called *yuloü*.[1] One day Coot (*potok*) and Falcon (*kevijiaruba*) had a race.[2] They started from Buena Vista Lake[3] up to *yuloü*. The one that got there first would own the rock. *Potok* swam up the river but *kevijiaruba* flew up the ridge and got there first so he owned it.

B.   CAPPANNARI (EMMA WILLIAMS: SADIE WILLIAMS)[4]

Two birds ran a race 'way above Kernville.[5] There is a big rock over there taller than a tree. They agreed that the first to get there would build his nest on the rock. *Kevixaraba* went across the mountains and *potok* ran along the river. *Kevixaraba* kept hitting the tops of the mountains and made the gaps you can see there today.[6] He won the race and had his nest on

------

[1]The location of this site is not clear, but if it is "near the beginning of the Kern River in the mountains," it would be considerably north of the Kawaiisu area.

[2]McCown adds this note: "*Kevijiaruba* lives in the mountains while *potok* lives on the ground in the water. *Potok* is a little black water bird that figures in the earth diving story. Probably this is Coot. *Kevijiaruba* is a little fellow like a chicken hawk. He lives in the mountains and is white colored. He is rare--not many of them." Informants had not identified either of the birds. In the 1970s no one seemed familiar with the word *potok*. The *keevižiyaribɨ*, however, was known to live in the mountains. The word would seem to be based on the stem *keevi* 'mountain'. One informant suggested that the bird could be a falcon.

[3]Buena Vista Lake, now used in an irrigation project, is southwest of Bakersfield. The race of the birds would have followed the course of the Kern River upstream.

[4]Cappannari begins the myth with a parenthetical note: "(The two birds, *kevixaraba* and *potok*, are unidentified.)."

[5]This location could conform to that given by McCown.

[6]This has reference to a single line of mountains with saddles in between the peaks.

the rock. *Potok* built his nest in the tules.

Kevixaraba walked down to South Fork. The people there were angry because he won the race. He knew they were waiting for him and he sang this song:

> *tuwunu tuwunu*
> *kinija su*
> *pavisa kedidi*
> *mun nanena*

Sadie Williams gave this translation: "What do you people think I am? A deer?"[7]

_____

[7]As the words of the song stand, they give no indication that they are in Kawaiisu.

44. Bat and Horsefly[1]

A.   ZIGMOND (EMMA WILLIAMS: ELSIE GARCIA)

Bat and Horsefly were brothers. Horsefly, the elder, had a wife and children.

The two brothers went hunting together. Horsefly saw a deer. He told Bat where it was, but Bat couldn't see it. Horsefly pointed at it and pointed at it, but Bat couldn't see it. Bat rubbed his eyes, but still he couldn't see it. Bat said, "Put me on your shoulder." Horsefly did, but still Bat couldn't see it. Horsefly put Bat down. Bat got some beaver-tail cactus [Opuntia basilaris][2] and rubbed his eyes with it. Then he saw the deer.

Bat told his brother to wait for him. He said he was going to kill the deer. He flew up and got on the deer's horns. He walked all over the horns. He kept looking for a spot where he could shoot him. He walked down his nose, his mouth, his chin. Finally he shot him below the neck. The deer was frightened and ran. Bat jumped off and went back to his brother. He told Horsefly he thought he missed the deer. His brother was angry. He said, "How could you miss him when you were on him?"

They tracked the deer and found it dead.[3] Bat pointed to the eyes and asked, "What are they for?" Horsefly said, "To see." Bat pointed to the ears. "What are they for?" "To hear." The nose. "What is it for?" "To smell with." The mouth. "What is it for?" "To eat with." The teeth. "What are they for?" "To chew with." The tail. "What is it for?" "To chase flies with." While they were talking, the deer got up and ran.[4] Horsefly was angry because the deer got away. He left Bat and went home.

---

[1]C. F. Voegelin (1935:199-200) includes this myth in his *Tübatulabal Texts*. Gayton refers to the Tübatulabal version in a personal communication (1937).

[2]The part of the cactus used is not specified here but it is clear in Cappannari's version, which does not identify the plant.

[3]As elsewhere in the myths, "dead" does not necessarily mean "dead."

[4]The last and most important question is omitted here probably because Elsie, the translator, a girl of about eighteen, was embarrassed by it. Sadie Williams, who translated for Cappannari ten years later, had no hesitancy in including it. It is also to be found in the Tübatulabal version.

Bat tracked the deer and found him. He carried him home.

It was getting dark. Horsefly's mother-in-law was worried about Bat. Bat came, left the deer outside, and went in the house. The house fire went out because of the flutter of Bat's wings. So they knew he had come in, but they couldn't see him.

Bat sat down beside the fire. He said he had brought the deer home. He told his brother to go out and bring it in. Horsefly tried to lift the deer, but he couldn't; it was too heavy. He came back and told Bat it was too heavy. Bat went out and brought the deer in.

Bat cooked some of the meat and they ate it. After eating, he wanted to dance. He told his brother to build a fire outside. At first Horsefly wouldn't do it, but the old woman told him to do as his brother said. And so he did.

Everyone went out to watch Bat dance. He danced with his bow and arrow in his hands. He sang: *napitat keetat koimi* [repeated].[5] As Bat danced and sang, he shot his brother, his brother's wife, the old woman (his brother's mother-in-law), and all the children except the youngest--a baby girl. The infant cried all night.

B.   CAPPANNARI (EMMA WILLIAMS: SADIE WILLIAMS)

Bat and Horsefly were brothers. Horsefly was the oldest; he had a wife and a little girl. Their mother, an old woman, lived with them.

The brothers went hunting together. Horsefly saw a big buck, but Bat couldn't see it. Horsefly turned his brother around until he was facing the buck, but still Bat couldn't see it. Then he rubbed his eyes with "stickers" [thistles that bear red flowers].[6] Now Bat could see the buck.

Bat said, "Watch me; I'll jump between his horns." He did so, and walked around looking for a good place to shoot him. He climbed on his ears, his eyelids, his nose, and then came down to his chin. Bat found a good place to shoot the buck. He shot it right in the follow of the neck and it fell down dead. Horsefly came up and asked his brother to name each part of the deer. Bat located and named his feet, mouth, and tail. Then he came to the buck's anus. He stuck his hand in there and the buck jumped up and ran away. Horsefly was mad at his brother and went home.

Bat chased the buck and killed him again. Bat carried the buck home and arrived there in the evening. He left the buck outside and went in. The fire went out just before he went in.[7] They built the fire again and found

_____

[5]No translation was provided.

[6]As the Kawaiisu name *navubɨ* indicates, the plant is a cactus and not a "thistle." The "stickers" would refer to the cactus thorns (spines).

[7]This statement seems to miss the point. There was no reason for the fire to go out *before* Bat went inside. The fire apparently went out

Bat hanging on the wall. Bat told his brother to build a fire outside.
He [Bat] said, "I'm mad. I'm going to dance and sing." They cooked the buck
and ate it. The mother, sister-in-law, and the little baby sat around the
fire while Bat and Horsefly danced. Bat took his bow and arrow and shot
Horsefly while he was dancing. Horsefly fell down and rolled on the ground.
The arrow broke when he rolled over. The old mother said, "Don't break your
brother's arrow." Bat then shot his mother. She fell down and never moved.
Bat saved the arrow and shot his sister-in-law with it. He took the little
baby into the brush house.

The baby cried, "Peep, peep, peep."

---

because of the fluttering of Bat's wings. See the Zigmond version.

45. Cottontail and the Sun[1]

A.

ZIGMOND (SETIMO GIRADO)

There is a stump of a tree in the ocean to the east. The sun slowly climbed up the stump. Cottontail, sitting by the edge of the ocean, watched the sun as it climbed up. Then he shot at it with his bow and arrow and hit it twice. The sun fell down into the ocean, and as it hit the water, made the sound [whispered] $k^wi\check{s}$ $k^wi\check{s}$ $k^wi\check{s}$.

Then Cottontail ran as fast as he could, carrying many arrows in the quiver on his back. He came this way. When the children saw him coming, they said, "Here comes the one who killed the sun!" Cottontail came to the children of Mountain Sheep. They were playing on a rock, and when they saw him coming, they said, "Here comes the one who killed the sun!" Cottontail came to the children of Antelope. They were playing on the ground, and when they saw him coming, they said, "Here comes the one who killed the sun!" They ran home. Cottontail followed them to the house of Antelope's mother.

Cottontail was hungry. The old woman told him to sit down. She gave him and her grandchildren tansy-mustard seeds [aka, *Descurainia* sp.] to eat. Cottontail mixed the *aka* with water and drank it. The children drank it, too. They ate so much that they were very full. Cottontail said, "Let's go and play on the see-saw." The children sat on one end and Cottontail on the other. He lifted them high and went very fast. They told him not to go so fast, but he didn't listen. Then he shook the log so that they all fell down and broke open. The *aka* seed came out of them.

Cottontail ran down the road. He came to a family that had a garden. He came at night and ate up everything in the garden. They found him there in the morning, and chased him with their dog. He ran and got into a rock pile. They wanted to kill him. Cottontail was sitting under the rocks. They tried to get him, but couldn't reach him. The rock pile had many holes. They crawled in to get him. He pushed the rocks on top of them and got out on the other side. He killed them all.

---

[1]There is a similar Chemehuevi myth outlined by Laird (1976:152ff.); an episode is listed here in the Introduction. Also note the Panamint tale "Cottontail and the Sun" included in this collection.

The sun was a person. He was sitting on a pole in the ocean shaking himself like a bird. Cottontail saw the sun and shot him with his bow and arrow. The sun went *sk ssh ssh* and it was dark.

Cottontail came this way. It was very dark. Mountain Sheep lived in brush houses and had children. The children saw Cottontail coming. They said, "Who killed the sun?" Cottontail was mad. He ate some *aka* [tansy-mustard seeds, *Descurainia* sp.] and the children ate some with him. Then the children were playing on their teeter-totter outside the house. Cottontail jumped on the teeter-totter and the children were dashed to the ground and killed.

Cottontail ran away and Mountain Sheep chased him. Cottontail hid under some rocks. They saw Cottontail come out from the other side of the pile of rocks. The rocks tumbled down the mountain and killed all of the Mountain Sheep.

It was dark for a whole week. Then the sun came out again.

---

[2]Cappannari calls this myth "The Sun (Tabi)."

46. Wildcat and "Man"[1]

A.   ZIGMOND (REFUGIA WILLIAMS)[2]

Wildcat was a hunter and he killed jackrabbits with just one arrow.
It had on it a white feather and white eagledown. He went every day to kill a
jackrabbit with it. On his way home he would gather twigs and lay them
around his pot to make a fire. He grew fat killing and eating a jackrabbit
every day.

One day he shot at a jackrabbit, but the arrow stuck in the rabbit
who ran off with it. Wildcat could see the arrow and followed it a long way,
but he finally lost track of it. He came back the next day and looked again,
but he couldn't find it. He kept looking. At last he saw the rabbit with
the arrow. He followed the rabbit all day long. Toward sunset the rabbit
was going through a hole in the sky. It dropped the arrow at the edge of the
hole and got away into another country.

Wildcat also entered the sky-hole and was going down a little canyon.
It was getting late. A cottontail ran across his path and under a rock. Wildcat killed it there with his arrow.[3] He took the cottontail and walked on
down the canyon. He saw a house with smoke coming out, and went inside. A
fire was burning and a man was lying with his back to the fire. Wildcat
started cooking the cottontail without disturbing the man. The man said, "That
wood worm[4] smells good!" Then he looked around and saw Wildcat. "Oh, it's
you, is it?" he said. Wildcat said, "Yes, I just killed a cottontail and I'm
roasting it." Wildcat invited the man to eat with him. The man said it
tasted good. He wanted to know what it was. He said he didn't know rabbits
were good to eat.

---

[1]As indicated in the Introduction, a similar tale is included in
the Chemehuevi myth "How Wildcat Brothers Recovered Their Hunting Song."
There too the occupant of the house is identified as a "man," but he is also
Sun Spider.

[2]For information about Refugia Williams, see note to "Coyote and
Red Racer."

[3]Obviously Wildcat recovered the arrow when the jackrabbit dropped
it.

[4]The Kawaiisu words here are *wovi ataavič(i)* literally meaning
'wood little tree worm'.

Every night the jackrabbits would come to this house to play the stick-hiding guessing game. They sang a song as they played: *hu?upi kamɨ we...ni*.[5] The game went on all night long every night.

The man got to thinking after finding that rabbit is good to eat. He and Wildcat planned to kill all the rabbits. They made a net. The rabbits came to play the game. The man and Wildcat put the net around the house. As the game went on, they went outside to set it up. Toward daylight the rabbits started to go home. They got tangled up in the net. Wildcat and the man hit them with clubs. They killed all of them. Next night more rabbits came and these were killed. Wildcat and the man kept doing this every night until all of them were killed. They dried the rabbitskins and hung them up. They ate all the rabbits they had and then began to eat the hides.

Man wanted Wildcat to go home. He took the net and made it into a rope. They went to the sky-hole. The man let the Wildcat down on the rope and told him to run around in a big circle when he reached the ground so that the man could tell that Wildcat had gotten down.

And so Wildcat got down and went home.

---

[5]The first two words of the song mean 'berries of the box thorn' (*Lycium andersonii*) and 'jackrabbit'.

47. The Giant Grasshopper[1]

A.   ZIGMOND (EMMA WILLIAMS: ELSIE GARCIA)

The giant Grasshopper *haakapainiži*[2] came from Nevada. He had a
large carrying basket, and went along on two long canes. As he went, he sang.
He came this way to hunt for little children.

There was a woman who was pounding acorns. Her little girl was playing nearby and crying. The mother told her daughter to go home, but she
wouldn't go. The mother became angry and went home alone. The girl stayed
and cried.

Haakapainiži came along. He spit[3] in his hand and held it out to
the little girl. "Grandchild," he said, "come get this fat." When she reached
for it, he caught her and put her in the basket on his back. He returned to
his home in Nevada. When he reached home, he ate the child.

Then he came back for a little boy. He caught the lad in the same
way. On the way home he passed under a tree. The boy seized hold of a

---

[1]It should be noted that Kawaiisu mythology distinguishes between
two man-eating monsters. One is *nɨhnɨhnoovi* who flies and carries people to
his distant home where he eats them. The other is *haakapainiži*, a giant grasshopper who walks along on two canes and is primarily interested in seizing
children. The same two monsters are to be found in the stories of other Great
Basin groups. Lowie (1924:75) records several Southern Ute tales about an
ogre who, like *haakapainiži*, has a basket in which to carry children. In one
story, a boy escapes by holding on to the limb of a tree under which the ogre
passes.

[2]Cf. the Kawaiisu-Chemehuevi myth parallels as listed in the Introduction. The Chemehuevi episode is similar to the one here relating to the
Quail Sisters. In both tales a Grasshopper is involved, though in the Chemehuevi tale he is referred to as an "old man," and as "*Haakapainiži* the giant"
in the Kawaiisu story. The giant's primary interest is in seizing and eating
children, so his behavior with the Quail Sisters is puzzling. A Kawaiisu
woman recalled that, when she was a child, her grandmother frightened her by
telling her, "*Haakapainiži* is coming!" (See Zigmond 1977:77.)
Gayton (personal communication 1937) suggested that the giant may "possibly
[be] a *very* alternated variant of [the] Walking Skeleton."

[3]This is an obvious euphemism. See Cappannari's version.

branch of the tree and hung there. The giant didn't notice. When he reached home, the boy wasn't in the basket.

One day *Haakapainiži* came this way again. The two Quail Sisters were walking along. Squirrel Hawk, the husband of one of them, told them not to sleep in a sandy wash because that was in *Haakapainiži*'s path. As they passed the wash, one of them said, "That would be a nice place to sleep." The other said that Squirrel Hawk had told them not to sleep there. But they slept there anyway.

Haakapainiži came along singing. The sisters heard him. He saw a dark object in the sand.[4] The sisters asked him what he was doing. He didn't answer. They asked him what he wanted. He said he wanted to sleep. They told him to sleep on the side of them. He said, "No." In between them? "No." On the other side of them? "No." At their feet? "No." At their heads? "Yes," he said; he would sleep there. The sisters asked him if he stretched. He said, "No." In the morning the sisters said he was very good not to have stretched. Just then he stretched and put out their eyes with his toes.[5] He left them. Soon Squirrel Hawk came. They told him their story.

Once *Haakapainiži* came to Mouse who lived with his family in a cave. Each member of the family had a hole. When they heard *Haakapainiži* coming, all the children ran into their holes. Just the parents stayed and waited. Mouse threw an arrow-straightener[6] into the fire. *Haakapainiži* came to the door. Mouse took hold of the hot stone. He told *Haakapainiži* to open his mouth and close his eyes tightly. Then he would throw one of his children into his mouth. *Haakapainiži* did as he was told. Mouse threw in the hot stone and he was killed.

At Inyokern, Mouse's cave and *Haakapainiži* turned to stone can still be seen.

B.   CAPPANNARI[7] (EMMA WILLIAMS: SADIE WILLIAMS)

A woman was pounding acorns near a spring. Her little daughter was

---

[4]Apparently the "dark object" was the sisters.

[5]Since he was a grasshopper, Laird's description (1976:166) is more appropriate: ". . . gouging out their eyes with the serrated undersides of his powerful legs."

[6]An arrow-straightener is a grooved rock which is heated and used to straighten arrows.

[7]Cappannari recorded four "Giant" myths--three from Emma Williams and one from Marie Girado. He calls them respectively "Giant," "Giant *Hakai Painiza*" (cf. Zigmond's *Haakapainiži*), "Giant," and "Giant Myth." *Haakapainiži*'s adventures were told as episodes of one story to Zigmond; Emma's account to Cappannari is treated as if there were separate tales. Furthermore, Zigmond's episodes 1 and 2 are merged into one in Cappannari's myth, so that the "little boy" is eliminated and the "little girl" escapes. Cappannari does not mention that the giant is a grasshopper.

crying nearby. This angered the mother so she took the acorns and went home.
She intended to come back for the child, but when she returned, the little
girl was gone.

The giant came up to the child and put some snot in his hand. He
said, "Come and eat this fat, my grandchild."[8] The child went to get the
fat, but it was just snot. The giant took her and put her in the basket on
his back. When he stooped under a limb, she climed out of the basket and hung
on to the limb. When the giant got home, she was gone.[9]

C.   CAPPANNARI (EMMA WILLIAMS: SADIE WILLIAMS)

Two Quails were sisters. One of them had a husband who was out
hunting. The Sisters were sleeping in the sand along the Giant's trail. He
had a long cane and they could hear him coming. He was singing. He came up
to them and they were afraid. They told him to sleep at their feet. He
wanted to sleep on the outside near one girl. "I am *Taünara*,"[10] he said.

Then they told him to sleep at their heads, and he slept there.
At daylight he stretched his feet and put out the eyes of both girls with his
toes. The Giant left them there. They were crawling around crying.[11]

D.   CAPPANNARI (EMMA WILLIAMS: SADIE WILLIAMS)

Several Mouse children lived in a cave. The mice had dug holes in
the corner of the cave. They heard the Giant coming. They put an oval piece
of obsidian in the fire. The Giant came in. He was singing, "*hakapem*, etc.,"
which means 'There is nobody in the canyon'.[12]

The Mouse father said, "Open your mouth and close your eyes, and
I'll throw a baby in." He threw the hot rock into the Giant's mouth. That
killed him.

That cave is at *supitabuve*, above Sand Canyon. In it is the Giant,
turned to rock.

---

[8]*Kaguci-* 'daughter's child' is the reciprocal of *kagu-* 'mother's
mother'.

[9]At this point Sadie Williams commented that one of her relatives
had visited Nevada and heard that the Giant stayed there. He lived on a rock
in the middle of a lake.

[10]Cappannari notes here: "No meaning to Sadie." The name is not
mentioned elsewhere.

[11]Comment by Sadie: "White people saw those giant tracks not long
ago on the other side of Death Valley."

[12]No meaning can be derived either from the native word or from the
"translation." *Hakapem* may be related to *Haakapainiži*.

The Giant[13] could walk from Inyokern to Onyx in one step.[14] One day he peeked into Coyote's cave. He was so big his rear end was far away.

Coyote's wife had many children. She heard the Giant coming so she heated a stone arrow-straightener[15] until it was red hot. The Giant had a lizard, and he cooked it over the fire that was burning in Coyote's place. He didn't notice the stone. After the lizard was cooked, he ate it. It wasn't enough. He wanted more to eat. Coyote's wife said, "I have many children. You can eat one. Close your eyes tight and I'll get you one." The first time, the Giant didn't close his eyes very tight. Coyote's wife said, "You must close your eyes very tight and open your mouth wide." Again he didn't close his eyes tight enough. The third time he closed his eyes real tight. She dropped the red-hot stone in his mouth. It landed in his stomach and he died.

This happened over at Panamint.

---

[13]Cappannari adds parenthetically here: "Term for giant is either *nɨkama* or *hakapainije*." The first word is not mentioned elsewhere, but note that a destructive character designated *nik^wama* is to be found in a Panamint myth included in this collection.

[14]The distance between Inyokern and Onyx is about 20 miles.

[15]See Footnote 6.

48. The Man-Carrying Bird[1]

A.   ZIGMOND (EMMA WILLIAMS: ELSIE GARCIA)

The hawk-like man-carrying bird *nɨhnɨhnoovi*[2] came from *aragawiiya* [Mt. Whitney][3] and went over to the coast to get men to eat.

A little man-bird, *nɨwɨbiči*,[4] lived around here. At night he would hear the *nɨhnɨhnoovi* flying over with the men he had caught. He tied a cord to a tree and made a loop on the ground. The next morning the *nɨwɨbiči* went to see if he had caught the great Bird in the trap.

The *nɨhnɨhnoovi* was there, but the *nɨwɨbiči* was afraid to go near. He kept walking around and around. He sang: *ɨnɨnɨnɨ ɨnɨnɨnɨ hiniyaro aniʔkʷiši kunsɨgi nuwuvidošo cowanomi*[5] [repeated]. He had an obsidian knife in the band around his head. He tried to get to the big Bird who watched him as he walked around. The *nɨwɨbiči* kept singing, but he came too close to the *nɨhnɨhnoovi*. The big Bird caught and swallowed him. Then the Man-Carrier got

---

[1]Similar tales about a man-carrying monster who takes his victims to his far-off home and eats them are to be found among Great Basin tribes. Sometimes, however, the would-be victim kills the monster--thus Lowie (1924: 112, 164) and Sapir (1930:464ff.).
    Gayton in a personal communication (1937) states: "[This] tale is somewhat comparable to [Great] Basin stories of Roc. The 'cutting way' out of a monster is a common Basin-Plateau episode."

[2]*noo-* to carry on one's back, 'pack'; cf. Southern Paiute *nɨnwɨnoovi* 'man-carrier, mythical bird that carries away people in his talons' (Sapir 1930:587); Chemehuevi *nɨnɨnoʔovi* 'mythic bird sp.' (Harrington 1969:20). The reduplicated form was used, but recent informants said that *nɨhnoovi* is also correct. According to Emma Williams, the bird doesn't flap its wings but sails along with wings outstretched. If it flapped its wings, it would blow houses down.

[3]Mt. Whitney, highest mountain in the United States, is considerably to the north of Kawaiisu territory.

[4]The little bird was not identified. The word *nɨwɨbi* means 'liver'; *nɨwɨ* is 'man, person'.

[5]No meaning was suggested. One informant thought that *kohoži* (Panamint, Western Shoshoni) words might be involved.

loose from the snare and flew home.

Every time the *nɨhnɨhnoovi* got home he would take a bath in a pond. The blood of men whom he killed can still be seen around the pond.

While still in the air, the *nɨwɨbiči* got out his knife and started cutting the *nɨhnɨhnoovi*'s heart-strings. When the strings were cut through, the big Bird dropped to the ground. The *nɨwɨbiči* climbed out through the *nɨhnɨhnoovi*'s mouth and came home.

B.   ZIGMOND (MARTINA COLLINS)

Coyote and Wolf were half-brothers. They had a lot of buckskin this side of Loraine. A hawk-like bird with large wings came from the east. Coyote made a trap to catch it. The bird got tangled in the trap. Coyote came to see. The bird seized Coyote, got loose, and flew back east with Coyote inside of him.

Coyote had a pipe[6] behind his ear. He used it to cut the bird's heart. The bird died and dropped into the ocean. Coyote made a bridge out of the bird's wings. He got back home, but he was grunting all the way home. He was sick. Wolf heard him as he came. Coyote had a light at the tip of his tail[7] and it showed him the way back.

When Coyote reached home, they had a big celebration with dancing and singing.

_____

[6]The 'pipe' was probably a section of 'cane' (*Phragmites australis*) used for smoking. When split lengthwise, a sharp edge is produced.

[7]The light at the end of Coyote's tail is mentioned in some versions of the story of the Bears at Walker Basin. Note also the relationship of Coyote's tail to his penis, indicated by Carobeth Laird (see Introduction).

49. The *Miitiipi*[1]

A.   <u>CAPPANNARI (MARIE GIRADO: CLARA GIRADO)</u>

The animal-people lived in brush houses[2] near each other. They went hunting together and always got what they went after. They always had deer meat and acorns to eat.

Falcon[3] killed a deer which fell near a river. He walked toward the deer he had just killed, and a Negro came out of the water. The Negro pulled the deer into the river. Falcon went home and said, "A *miitiipi* pulled it [the deer] in."[4] The same thing happened at least three times when he went hunting.

Falcon's family started to get hungry. Coyote got mad. He said, "Leave it to me. I'll take care of that *miitiipi*. I'll kill him." While Coyote watched, the same thing happened. Coyote was so angry he jumped up and down, and started shooting. He shot that colored man and he dropped dead. He walked up to the dead one and found that it was a large black lizard.[5]

---

[1]Cappannari calls this tale "Origin of Negroes," obviously because of the reference to a Negro and because of Marie Girado's final comment: "That meant there was going to be colored people." But this overlooks the meaning of *miitiipi*: an undesirable sight which portends bad luck or disaster, such as a rattlesnake, grizzly bear, or non-Indian. See Zigmond (1977:77).

[2]Cappannari repeatedly records 'bush house' instead of 'brush house', but the latter constitutes a more accurate description.

[3]Cappannari gives the Kawaiisu name but notes that it refers to an 'unidentified bird'. McCown identifies it as a falcon.

[4]The Kawaiisu equivalent is given. I correct it thus: *miitiipi igatiik^w eenaneena.*

[5]The animal, *wogosinazi*, was described as a "large black lizard with a blue-green belly" and also as a "black lizard that climbs trees."

50. Owl's Wife[1]

A.   ZIGMOND (SETIMO GIRADO)

Owl lived in a winterhouse with his wife Snowbird[2] and a little daughter. Owl went hunting rabbits. Snowbird was hungry. Owl would catch a rabbit and eat it by himself. Snowbird was angry. She gathered the bones lying about, broke them up, and while Owl was out hunting, stuck them with the points upward in the snow at the door of the house. Owl came home with many rabbits to cook. They were hanging at his waist. When Owl tried to scrape his feet, the bones stuck into them, but he felt nothing because his feet were frozen from the cold. Snowbird said to herself, "I have him now."

When Owl's feet grew warm, they began to pain him. He said, "My feet hurt. Look at my feet." His wife pushed the bones in farther. By morning his feet had swelled up so that he couldn't go hunting. "I'm very sick," he said. "I'm going to die. Put little horns[3] like mine on our child." Owl died. Snowbird twisted the hair [of the child] and tied it up to form horns.

Snowbird left there and went along the road with the child on her back. In a house there was an old lady making a carrying-basket. She had a son. Snowbird came there. The old lady said, "I have a very bad son." "I will help you make the basket," Snowbird said. The old lady said, "You had better go away before my boy comes." Snowbird made a little of the basket and then left.

The boy was Skunk. He came home and saw that part of the basket was made by Snowbird. He smelled someone strange. "Who made that?" he asked. "I did," said the old lady. "No one was here." Skunk didn't believe her. "You lie," he said. He went around to find the tracks. He went around and around but couldn't find any. He came home again. "You have her here," he said. "It smells good." Skunk went out again to find the tracks. He looked around the rocks, the trees; he smelled everywhere. He found the tracks. "I'm

---

[1]Lowie, in his *Shoshonean Tales* (1924), gives three versions of this myth: "Owl's Wife," "Owl's Widow," and "The Travels of Owl's Widow." Carobeth Laird (1974) refers to a similar Chemehuevi myth which is concerned with the Great Horned Owl.

[2]The bird is not identified, but the Kawaiisu name *nɨvarookɨzi* is apparently built on the stem *nɨva-* 'snow'.

[3]Horn(s) *aapɨ*; diminutive *aapɨzi*.

going to track her. I'll catch her somewhere," he said.

Snowbird was going slowly carrying the baby. Skunk caught up with her. He said to himself, "I'll copulate with her." The woman refused. She said, "There are mountain sheep over there; go hunt." Skunk took his bow and arrow, and went away.

Snowbird had a rabbitskin blanket. She put it over a yucca pole. It looked like her. Skunk looked back and thought she was there. He came back and approached the blanket. "I'm going to have her now," he said. He put his arm around the blanket. "Now I'm going to do it," he said. It scratched him. "Oh no, don't do that," he said. The woman was far away. Skunk took off the blanket and saw it wasn't her. He cried with anger. He looked around for her tracks. He broke wind down the road.[4] It was like a fog. The smell reached the woman and she died. The little daughter was sitting there alone.

Badger came out and found the dead woman and the child. He looked at the mother and saw that she was pretty. He looked around and said, "Who killed this woman? I'm a doctor. I have a song to make her well. She will get well quickly." He sang: "*huna?ina huna?ina hari?ina hari?ina tiviši?ani tiviši?ani tubokiva tubokiva.*"[5] He circled around and blew on her. Pretty soon her fingers moved. He danced. The woman got up. Badger said, "Now I must give you something to make you well." He copulated with her.

Snowbird went on a long way to a big rancheria where there were many people: Chicken Hawk, Squirrel Hawk, Falcon, Eagle, Quail, Crow, Buzzard, Bluejay, Horned Toad, and others. Snowbird said, "I'll go there." She sang: "*nuk^wipagi nuk^wipagi sinava?aduwami.*"[6] She came to the rancheria and stayed there overnight. Coyote lived there. He said, "Whoever is a good hunter will marry this woman." Next morning everyone got his bow and arrow and started to hunt. Coyote had a tame rabbit which he took along into the field. He killed it and came back and said, "I have made the first kill. I'm going to marry her." Snowbird didn't like him and didn't want him.

Chicken Hawk and Falcon were brothers who lived on a rock. Snowbird liked Chicken Hawk and went to live with him. Falcon was jealous and angry. He tossed a sifting tray into the air and told it to bring back wind. He said, "Come, good strong wind, pull out brush and everything!" He sang:

---

[4]Setimo Girado rendered the Kawaiisu word *huu-* 'urinated'. However, the usual meaning is 'to break wind' and the stem has the same meaning in Southern Paiute and Chemehuevi. Perhaps there is a special implication in the word when applied to skunks. In one of Lowie's myths (1924:179) there is this passage: "Skunk . . . broke wind as he did when angry. The child looked back and said, 'There is rain coming over there.' 'No, Skunk has broken wind.' The wind caught them by a dry lake and being unable to breathe they died."

[5]The Kawaiisu word for badger is *huna-*. However, Elsie Garcia, who looked over the myth at a later time, said that the song is in the Tübatulabal language.

[6]The words of the song apparently mean 'run-walk, run-walk to your uncle (i.e., your mother's younger brother)'.

"wokotɨbɨni paikinu"[7] [repeated]. A whirlwind came and blew everything and everyone except Horned Toad. He held on, and the horns on his head were formed when the sand and stones passed over him.

---

[7]The words of the song are translated: 'My tray, come back (or home)!' The word *wokotɨbɨ* is usually defined as 'the rim of a twined basket', but here it is said to refer to a flat basket tray resembling a *saguci* (a flat tray of coiled weave).

51. Eagles Rescue a Man

A. CAPPANNARI (EMMA WILLIAMS AND MARIE GIRADO)[1]

Every year a *kohoži*[2] man used to climb a cliff to reach an eagle's nest. It was a sheer cliff and at the top he had to walk along a high, narrow ledge to the nest.

One year he arrived at the nest but then was afraid to go back. Maybe it was the eagle that made him afraid. He stayed there for two weeks or more without food or water. The mother eagle brought jackrabbits to its two babies. The man was very thirsty and drank the rabbits' blood. Then he dried the rabbits and ate them.

His relatives kept looking for him. Every day they came to the foot of the cliff to see him. He was getting as thin as a skeleton.

The baby eagles grew larger. Every day the man talked to them. He said to them, "Don't leave me." When they were old enough to fly, he got into his net and tied an eagle to each side of it. He told the eagles to take him to the opposite hill.

They flew him down safely. The man kept his eyes shut while they were flying. When they reached the ground, he opened his eyes. He turned the eagles loose and they flew back to their nest.

The man returned home. He was so thin, he looked like an *ʔinɨpi* [ghost].

His relatives wept.[3] They pounded some *kuʔu* seeds [*Mentzelia* sp.] into a paste that looks like peanut butter.[4] They rubbed this on his body

---

[1]Cappannari adds this note: "In 1947 Emma told me the following semi-legendary account of a Panamint [man] who went after an eagle. The following summer Marie [Girado] told me the same tale. The two versions were almost identical."

[2]Both Cappannari and I identified the *kohoži* as 'Panamint'; i.e., Western Shoshoni. However, our consultants never used an English equivalent.

[3]Presumably they wept at seeing his emaciated appearance.

[4]Several species of *Mentzelia* (stickseed, blazing star) yield seeds

because his skin was so burned.

---

which are an important food source. When pounded, the seeds express oil
which converts them to the consistency of peanut butter. This quality is
mentioned in several myths.

52. Rat and Deer (The Hoodwinked Dancers)[1]

A.   ZIGMOND (SETIMO GIRADO)

Deer lived in the mountains. Rat said to them, "Come down and let's dance." Deer came down. The little fawns came first. Bat wanted the big deer to come down. They came. Rat danced with the deer all night.

Rat held the sharp-pointed leaf of yucca in his hand. He said, "All of you shut your eyes." As soon as they closed their eyes, he stuck one of them with the yucca point and killed him. (The yucca leaf was Rat's arrow. The brown color at its point is deer's blood.) But one deer kept his eyes open. The deer went back up the mountain. Rat said to himself, "I'm going to burn [i.e., roast] him in the morning."

The next morning the deer saw smoke come out of Rat's house. "He has already burned him up," they said. But Rat was burning brush. Then he ate the deer.

Rat called the deer down again the next night. Deer came down. They were going to kill Rat with their horns this time. They danced. Toward morning Rat took his arrow. He told them to shut their eyes, but they watched. As he was about to pierce a buck, the buck turned and pierced him with his horns. Rat died. "Rat is no more," they said. They discovered that he was a rat.

Then the deer went up over all the mountains.

B.   CAPPANNARI (MARIE GIRADO)

Rats gave a party. They invited lots of people. Some fawns came first. Rats told the fawns to go home. "We don't want children," they said. Soon large deer came. They had antlers.

All the deer were dancing. They danced all night. Early in the

---

[1]Lowie (1924:18) records a similar tale which he calls "Rat." The narrator is Southern Ute. Rat's guests are not limited to deer but include antelope, deer, elk, mountain sheep. Thompson (1929:295) provides a bibliography for stories of this type.

morning Rats said, "You fellows close your eyes." While their eyes were closed, Rats took knives [the yucca spines which have red tips] and stuck them into one of the deer. He fell down. The rest of the deer went home. Rats said, "We're going to burn that deer."[2]

Every night they did the same things and each night Rats killed one deer. Pretty soon the deer figured out what was happening. They killed the rats with their horns.

---

[2]Marie explained that the rats told the deer that they were going to burn the dead one but they really intended to make jerky of him.

53. A Visit to the Underworld

A.

ZIGMOND (EMMA WILLIAMS:[1] ELSIE GARCIA)

Long ago there was a man who was sick. There was a worm in him. To cure himself, he drank *moopɨ* [jimsonweed], swallowed *taasuʔuvɨ* [red ants], and applied nettles to his skin. He lay in the sun. But none of it did him any good. There was nothing left for him to do except to visit *Yahwera*'s House [*yaahʷeʔera kahniina*] underground. It is reached through a hole going down in a mountain in Back Canyon. Sometimes the opening can be seen, but sometimes there are only rocks there. That's where the spirits of killed deer go.

The man joined two nets together and tied one end around his waist. He told his friends that if he got to the botton, the nets would be loose. If they were still tight, he hadn't yet reached the bottom. The friends tested the combined nets. They were loose. And so the men pulled them back.

He began to walk through a tunnel. He stumbled over a large snake [*kogo*, a gopher snake]. He climbed over it. Farther along he came to a great snake [*tugubaziitɨbɨ*].[2] He climbed over it. Then there was a brown bear [*moʔoriiži*] roaring. He passed it by. He came to a big grizzly bear [*pogʷitɨ*] growling. He went past it. Then he didn't see any other animals.

He kept walking. He came to a big tree where deer had been. He could hear rocks making the noise of deer. Passing by, he came finally to where *Yahwera* was. *Yahwera* wore a mountain quail feather blanket.[3] He asked the man what he was doing there. The man said he was sick and wanted to get well. But *Yahwera* knew all about his illness without being told. *Yahwera* gave him some acorn mush in an acorn cupule and a little dried deer meat. The sick man didn't think it would be enough for him, but when he took some, the

---

[1]Emma Williams told this story when, after giving a vague description of the human afterworld (*ɨnɨpita kahniina* 'Ghost's House'), she said she could tell me something of the afterworld of deer.

[2]The *tugubaziitɨbɨ* is a large supernatural snake that is an unlucky omen when it appears in the sky. The *kogo* seems not to have any evil connotation.

[3]*Yahwera* is apparently associated with mountain quail--see the "*Yahwera* Takes a Wife" myth. But he is also described as looking "like a hawk. One hears it, but doesn't see it. It imitates a man talking, a dog barking, and so on."

same amount was left. He couldn't eat it all. When he couldn't eat any more, he gave the cupule back to *Yahwera*.

Yahwera then told him to come with him into another room. There the man saw the horns of all the deer that had been killed and the arrows with which they had been shot. *Yahwera* said that the deer were not really dead. The deer that the man had heard along the tunnel were the deer that had been "killed."

Yahwera took the man to the place where he kept medicine. *Yahwera* asked him which one he wanted; he named them all. Then *Yahwera* came to the songs and named them--the round-dance song, the doctor's song, and many others. There was the stick-hiding guessing game song apparently used in curing.[4] But the sick man selected another song which accompanies a dance, *muguwaatɨvivi*.[5]

The man was ready to return home. He wondered which way to go. If he went back the way he came, there would be no one to pull him up. *Yahwera* told him to keep on going to the other end, and when he was out, to sing his song for three nights, and not to tell anyone where he got the song. He was instructed to go to the spring above the Piute Rancheria. *Yahwera* said he was no doctor, but that if the sick man wanted to get well, he would have to go to the spring, build a fire in the sweathouse, take a bath, and wash his hair.

The sick man did as he was told. He kept along the tunnel and came out at Loraine.[6] He came to the spring and made a fire in the sweathouse. *Yahwera* had told him that he would feel the worm coming out, but not to touch it until it was actually on the way out. The man felt it, pulled it out, and threw it into the fire. It had come out at the knee. Then he went to the people who lived around there. They knew he had been sick and wondered why he had come so far from where he lived. He said he wasn't doing anything--just visiting. They tried to give him blankets to sleep in as a guest, but he said he didn't want them. He would build a fire and sleep by it.

He built the fire and sang all night. In the morning a woman asked him where he got the song that made them feel like dancing. He wouldn't answer. He slept all day and sang all night for three nights. People thought it strange because they had never heard of his knowing any songs. On the morning after the third night, he told his whole story. After that he was well. He went back to Kelso Valley where he had come from.

He wasn't sick any more.

The grandmother of Emma Williams [the informant] had seen the man and told Emma the story.[7]

------

[4]This song is mentioned in the "Wildcat and 'Man'" myth, but there it has no reference to curing.

[5]The word *muguwaatɨ* refers to "craziness" and here perhaps indicates a distinctive type of dance.

[6]Loraine and the Piute Rancheria are about five or six miles apart. Both were old village sites.

[7]Although Emma considered the story "non-mythical," the mythical

This happened long ago.

Many people lived in Back Canyon. A man went from there to *Yahwera*'s Hole (*yaah^weʔera toʔowiina*) which is by the place called *cug^wamɨhavaʔadɨ*.[8] He didn't eat for three days, but sat by the hole. He ate tobacco (*soʔodɨ*)[9] and got drunk on it. At the hole there was a rock that opened and closed.[10] He waited, and at one moment when the rock opened, he slipped through quickly and went in. Near the mouth of the hole he saw arrows. These are the arrows by which deer were killed. The deer leave them here when they go inside. The man passed by, but soon he saw a snake, a rattlesnake as big as a log. He couldn't get past at first, but he watched it a long time and then stepped over it. Then he met a huge grizzly bear, but he went on. He was deep in the hole.

He heard noises that sounded "like a train." He listened, and then saw two old men.[11] They said, "What do you want? What are you looking for?" They gave him one pinyon in a winnowing basket. He ate the pinyon, but every time he ate one, another was there. He was hungry and ate many, but there was always one left. There were all kinds of games there. The old men said, "Take your choice," but he didn't want any. He took a curing song.

The two men were deer. There were many deer around. The visitor stayed there a year. The old men told a boy (a young deer) to show him the way out. It was not the same as the way he had come in. The boy went ahead, and the man followed. The man saw water that was like a window. He could see the mountains through it. But it wasn't water. He passed through it and did not get wet. When he was outside, he looked back and saw the "water" again. Before he left, the boy told him that for three days he was not to tell people where he had been. "If you tell," the boy said, "the grizzly bear will kill you."

The man went home and sang in the evening. It was a good song, and the people liked it. On the second night he sang again. People wanted to know where he got the song. They kept asking until he was tired of being questioned, and he told them. He was angry because they bothered him. He told them everything about the hole, about the rock that opened and closed, about

---

elements are clear and obvious. *Yahwera* is a supernatural creature (see Zigmond 1977). The inexhaustible food supply is common to all the versions recorded, and is characteristic of tales of the "other world" and the "visit to the dead" of other cultures. Cf. Thompson (1929:335), Kroeber (1907:228), and Lowie (1924:106, 123, 132, 153).

[8]The site is near a mountain between Loraine and Kelso Valley.

[9]This is the preferred tobacco, *Nicotiana bigelovii*. Another species, *N. attenuata*, is weaker and less desirable.

[10]Setimo demonstrated the action by placing the palms of his hands together and rhythmically separating them.

[11]*Yahwera* is not mentioned except in connection with the name of the "hole."

the rattlesnake and the grizzly bear, about the noise he had heard. He said, "They asked me what I wanted. I got that song from them. The boy brought me out, but he told me not to tell for three days."

The next morning he went in the canyon. He met the grizzly bear who ate his head off.

C.   ZIGMOND (EMMA WILLIAMS: SADIE WILLIAMS)[12]

In Kelso Valley there lived a man who was always sick. Something was growing in his stomach; it made his stomach swell.[13] To cure himself he took jimsonweed, swallowed red ants, and walked naked through nettles. He didn't get any better. Then he went to Back Canyon where there is a hole in the mountain. It is the entrance to *Yahwera*'s house.

They tied three nets end to end, and bound one end around his waist to let him down slowly. "If I get down," he said, "I'll shake the net." He reached the botton. They pulled up the nets and went home.

The man saw a tunnel through white rock. He walked along and came to a big gopher-snake stretched across his path. He climbed over it. This snake was the "door" to *Yahwera*'s house. A little farther on he came to a large rattlesnake [*tugubaziitɨbɨ*]--bigger than the gopher-snake [*kogo*]. He passed a brown bear and a grizzly bear who growled at him. He walked on.

He came to *Yahwera*'s house. There was a light inside and a large mountain mahogany bush [*sɨnaʔaruubɨ, Cercocarpus betuloides*] with many deer eating the leaves.[14] Then he came to *Yahwera* who asked him, "What's the matter?" The man told him he was sick, but *Yahwera* said, "I know why you came." He told the man to sit down and gave him acorn mush in an acorn cupule, and a little dried deer meat. The man ate some, but he couldn't eat it all. *Yahwera* put the rest away.

The man said, "I want medicine." *Yahwera* asked, "What kind?" There were all kinds of medicines wrapped in deer hide in one room. Each one was named. The man decided not to take a medicine. Instead, he took a curing song. *Yahwera* said, "I'm not a doctor, but there is a big doctor at *ševɨbozɨgadɨ*, the spring above the Piute Rancheria."[15] The song was wrapped up in deer skin like the medicines. Yahwera told him to go out another way and he would come to the spring. The man passed the grizzly bear, the brown bear, the rattle-snake, and the gopher snake.[16]

---

[12]Emma told me this tale twice: in 1936 Elsie Garcia was the translator; in 1937, Sadie Williams.

[13]According to the end of the story, there is a worm inside him.

[14]Ernest C. Twisselmann notes in his *Flora of Kern County, California* (p. 255), "Mountain mahogany is an important browse plant for livestock and deer."

[15]While in both the 1936 and 1937 versions which Emma Williams narrates, the "man" is told that he will find a "doctor" at the spring near the Piute Rancheria, no doctor actually appears.

[16]Even though the man may have left the underworld "another way,"

At the spring there was a sweathouse. The man built a fire, took a bath, washed and combed his hair. He went to a nearby house and ate. He built a fire outside at night and sang all night. He sang three nights. The worm came out of his upper leg. He pulled it out, threw it in the fire, and jumped away. He got well.

D.   CAPPANNARI (MARIE GIRADO: CLARA GIRADO)[17]

A man was up at the cave above Indian Creek. He ate a large piece of tobacco without lime[18] because he wanted luck. After he ate the tobacco, the entrance to the cave closed.[19] He began to walk through the tunnel which had no end. He was very frightened. He saw many different animals--deer, bear, etc. They were Kawaiisu and spoke just like people. Someone handed the man a basket with one pinyon in it. He ate the pinyon, but there was another one there. He was also given a never-emptying basket with one acorn in it.

There were many different kinds of luck on the cave walls. He saw a bow and arrow of a good hunter in a prominent place, and the bows and arrows of inferior hunters in subordinate positions. He took something for his luck.[20] Finally he came to the end of the cave. He saw water that was transparent like a window. He came out through the water and found that he was 'way up in Back Canyon.[21]

The man had been gone a whole year. His relatives didn't know where he had been.

---

he seems to have passed in reverse order the same animals as before.

[17]Cappannari calls this tale "Legend." Since he did not obtain a version from Emma Williams, he could not have understood its broader aspects. Marie's narrative shows a relationship with the one I had recorded from her husband Setimo ten years earlier.

[18]Tobacco was regularly chewed with slaked lime. Eating the tobacco without lime must have produced a stronger reaction.

[19]Presumably he was already inside the cave.

[20]No reference is made to "illness," but perhaps this is implied by his seeking "luck."

[21]Cappannari notes parenthetically that the place in Back Canyon is "a few miles from the cave entrance."

54. *Yahwera* Takes a Wife[1]

A.

ZIGMOND (SETIMO GIRADO)

This is a true story.

Many people lived in the rancheria at Canebrake.[2] A little girl
was angry at her mother and was crying. The mother was making acorn mush[3]
at a spring near there. She left the girl and took the mush home. Then the
mother said, "I'll go get her now." The mother came back but the little
girl was gone. The mother looked all around, but couldn't find her tracks.
She returned home and told the other people. Everyone went out to look, but
they couldn't find the girl. They looked for a year and a half.

Yahwera[4] had taken the girl away. He took her into that big rock
where he lived.[5] He fed her mountain quail which he cooked by putting them
under his arm. In a year the girl grew up and was his wife. Sometimes she
went outside to gather the leaves and flowers of the tickseed plant [*Coreopsis
bigelovii, tɨhɨvidɨbɨ*].[6] Her brother was out hunting deer. He saw the girl

---

[1]This tale closely parallels one told by the neighboring Tübatulabal, "*Yihawal* Steals Girl" (Voegelin 1935:207).

[2]For the location of this site, see John Marcus' version.

[3]To be edible, acorns are prepared through three successive steps:
they are pounded into meal which is leached (through several pourings of
water) and cooked to mush. It would seem more likely that the leached meal
would be taken home for cooking.

[4]The supernatural creature *yaah^we?era*--which I have anglicized to
Yahwera--seems to appear in various forms, but principally as a bird. He is
said to imitate the sounds made by different animals and birds. See the tale
"A Visit to the Underworld" and the account in *The Supernatural World of the
Kawaiisu* (1977). *Yahwera* is somehow linked with mountain quail.

[5]His dwelling is underground, reached through an entrance-way in
the rocks. The problem of getting into it is described in the "Underworld"
tale.

[6]Tickseed is an important spring food plant. The leaves (some informants say the flowers also) are picked and eaten raw. They may also be
cooked (see the *Kawaiisu Ethnobotany*).

181

eating the *tɨhɨvidɨ*. She wore a dress made of mountain-quail feathers. He went home and told his parents, "I saw my sister out there." He had recognized his sister even though she was big.

The girl was pregnant. *Yahwera* took her to her home. "Take care of my baby," he told her. He came to her at night. He killed a large deer and gave it to his mother-in-law. He returned to his place and left his wife at her home. The next evening he came again. There was a big fire there. When he came to his wife, he touched her foot with his, and the fire went out. He told her that would happen.[7] He warned her that for three days she was not to tell where she had been.

The next morning her babies were born. They were mountain quail. They were all around the sunhouse. She couldn't catch them. Then she told where she had been. That is why her children ran away. The quail went up on the mountain and threw rocks at the people. They killed everyone. They were little *Yahwera*s. They went to their father in the rocks.

B.   ZIGMOND (JOHN MARCUS)

At Canebrake[8] a woman was leaching acorn meal.[9] Her daughter, about six or seven years of age, was with her, but the little girl was angry. Her mother said, "Let's go home." The daughter said, "I won't go home." She lay down on the ground and wouldn't move. The mother went home without her. The little girl didn't come home and pretty soon her mother went back to fetch her. The mother couldn't find her. She looked all around, but she couldn't see any tracks. She kept looking every day, but she found no trace of her daughter. The *Yahwera* had come and carried her away.

That was in the winter. In the spring the girl's brother was out deer-hunting and he saw his sister eating tickseed leaves.[10] She had a blanket of mountain-quail feathers around her. *Yahwera* had given it to her. She was pregnant. The brother said, "We're going to have a celebration at home."[11] His sister said she would come.

The boy went home and told his mother that he had found his sister who would come when they had the celebration. The girl came as it was getting dark when no one could see her. She stayed overnight, and the next night she

---

[7]The relevance of this episode is not clear.

[8]Canebrake Creek, though usually dry, flows into the South Fork of the Kern River. It takes its English name from the presence of "cane," carizzo grass (*Phragmites australis*) which Lt. R. S. Williamson reported in 1853 (Twisselmann 1967:180). The plant is no longer to be found there.

[9]This is the second step in making acorns edible. See Footnote 3.

[10]It was the proper season. Tickseed leaves are eaten in the spring.

[11]No reason for the celebration is given.

gave birth. The babies kept coming one after the other "maybe every five minutes." They looked like mountain quail. She put them in a sack. They filled the sack. *Yahwera* told her to be sure to close the sack tight and tie it so that they couldn't get out.

Coyote came to the girl and said he wanted to see the babies.[12] She said, "*Yahwera* told me to keep the sack closed." Coyote kept insisting, and finally she opened the sack. All the babies jumped out and scattered all around. Coyote tried to catch them, but he couldn't get one. They ran back to *Yahwera*'s place. *Yahwera* was very angry. He took stones and threw them at all the people. He killed them all.

---

[12]Coyote is not mentioned in Setimo Girado's version of this myth. However, Coyote's insistence upon looking into a closed container is a common episode. Compare the "Coyote and the Basket" tale and the accompanying footnotes.

55.   Quail Learns about Cradle-Making

A.   ZIGMOND (EMMA WILLIAMS: ELSIE GARCIA)

Long ago Quail used to make cradles out of Sandbar willow [*Salix hindsiana*]. But all her infants died.

Quail has a black face because of her weeping.

She wondered why her children died. Then she stopped using Sandbar willow, and instead used Red willow [*Salix laevigata*] and Arroyo willow [*Salix lasiolepis*] out of which to make cradles. The children didn't die any more.

That is why Sandbar willow is never used for cradles. Only Red willow and Arroyo willow are utilized for this purpose.

56. Dove

A. CAPPANNARI (EMMA WILLIAMS: SADIE WILLIAMS)

Dove's husband died. She stayed with her mother-in-law and pounded acorns. She rubbed her legs with red clay and that is why Dove's legs are red now. Her bedrock mortar became stained with red. It can be seen in Kelso Valley.

Dove painted her legs red because she wanted another husband, but when her mother-in-law asked her why she painted her legs, she got angry and went away.

57. Why Dogs Are Dumb

A.   ZIGMOND (SETIMO GIRADO)

A man was having sexual intercourse with his wife. Dog saw them. "Dirty!" said Dog. Coyote said, "Dog is bad." He [Coyote] didn't like it. "We will sew up his mouth," said Coyote. "He won't say it any more."

B.   CAPPANNARI (CLARA GIRADO)

In the old days dogs would often watch people while they were having sexual intercourse. Once a dog said to such a couple, "You are doing a very nasty thing." The couple were angry at the dog. They said, "You always tell people about the things you see." The woman said, "I will sew your lips together so you won't tell any more."

That is why, today, dogs can't talk.

C.   ZIGMOND (EMMA WILLIAMS AND JOHN NICHOLS)

A *kohoži* man[1] was hunting. He killed a deer and made camp. He had a dog with him. The man was cutting up the meat. He asked the dog, "How are we going to eat it? Shall we roast it?" The dog said, "You didn't ask me this morning when you had your meal." People said, "We're going to die because the dog talked."[2] The next morning they found the man dead.

That's all the dog said.

---

[1]The *kohoži* were northeast neighbors of the Kawaiisu.

[2]The talking of a dog is mentioned as one of the ominous signs (*tuuwaruugidɨ*). See Zigmond (1977:61).

189

58.   Rattlesnake and King Snake

A.

ZIGMOND (BERTHA GOINGS)

Rattlesnake and King Snake challenged each other as to which was the meanest. King Snake swallowed Rattlesnake. That is why King Snake is poisonous but has no rattles.

59. The Slide in Jawbone Canyon

A.

ZIGMOND (ANDY GREENE)

Chipmunk wanted to kill bighorn sheep. He was on a mountain over-looking Jawbone Canyon, and he saw bighorn sheep down below. To get down quickly, he slid all the way down the side of the canyon and made a trail as he dragged his tail.

You can see the trail to this day.[1]

---

[1]The narrator, Andy Greene, has pointed out to me this slide from the opposite side of the canyon. It is a narrow bare trail going straight down the mountainside.

60. An Incident in Kelso Valley

A.
CAPPANNARI (MARIE GIRADO?)

Over on the other side of Sageland,[1] on the ridge, a snake came down to the creek to get water. When she went back, she was very angry and walked zigzag. She turned into bushes which are still there--they can be seen from Kelso Valley. Those bushes are called *hunuvɨ*.[2] They make a medicine which is bitter and is taken to relieve menstrual cramps.

B.
CAPPANNARI (EMMA WILLIAMS)

Several women came down to get water at the creek. They were birds. Then they went back toward a ridge. They heard someone shouting, so they stopped. It was Coyote. The women turned into rocks. They are still there.

C.
ZIGMOND (ANDY GREENE)

Not far from Sageland, Rattlesnake was coming down to the water. Some people were coming down for water from the opposite side. Coyote hollered, and the people turned to rock. So did Coyote. They are still there. Rattlesnake's diamond-shaped pattern can be seen in the way the bushes grow there.

----

[1]During the mining era of the last century, Sageland was a flourishing town in Kelso Valley. Today a bronze plaque marks the site.

[2]Desert bitter-brush, *Purshia glandulosa*, *hɨnavɨ*, has medicinal usages mentioned in the *Kawaiisu Ethnobotany*.

61. The Bridge in Kelso Canyon[1]

A.

ZIGMOND (MARTINA COLLINS)

There is a rock which protrudes from the mountainside in Kelso Canyon. It is called Star Rock.[2]

Long ago little rock-birds[3] were building a bridge across Kelso Canyon to Nichols Peak. The Big Hawk[4] didn't want the bridge. He struck at it with his claws and broke it to pieces. The broken stones of the bridge are still to be seen scattered about there. Only the protruding rock remains where it was.

---

[1]The Tübatulabal also have a story of the attempt to build a bridge "from the top of the mountains across the valley to Nichols Peak" (Voegelin 1938:40). Nichols Peak must have been close to the "border" of the Kawaiisu and Tübatulabal areas and was, of course, familiar to both peoples. Large "broken" rocks in the vicinity must have provided the basis for the tale.

[2]It is not clear whether this is a popular or Kawaiisu name. No basis for the name was given.

[3]*Cigiʔivɨ* was identified as 'rock bird' by some informants and as 'cactus wren' by others.

[4]This may have been one of the mythical birds, but I failed to record its Kawaiisu name.

62. A Tale of Tobacco

A.

McCOWN[1] (SANTOS PHILLIPS)

There was a person--had no mother or father. Went around the world and fell down. They took him to the chief. Coyote talked to him but he would not answer. Whirls around. Coyote says: "I know him. You are *so?od* [tobacco]." No father and no mother.[2] (*supuhupaik*--no more).[3]

B.

McCOWN (RAFAEL GIRADO)

So?oda was a man. He had no mother. He is definitely personified. But jimsonweed (*mop*) is not personified. It is always a plant.[4]

C.

ZIGMOND

One night in the winterhouse they heard a noise something like the buzzing of a bee. They went outside and saw this hardened tobacco juice. It was a little black thing on the ground. They asked it who it was but it wouldn't say anything. This happened several nights. It didn't say anything. Coyote didn't go out, but he said he would go the next night. They heard the

---

[1]McCown calls this tale "A Scrap of a Myth about Tobacco." It is here reproduced just as it appears in his fieldnotes. Had he prepared it for publication, he would probably have used complete sentences. While it may be "a scrap of a myth," the fact that it has been recorded as an independent incident five times may indicate that it is complete in itself.

[2]At this point McCown comments: "This is evidently a scrap from something. Santos Phillips made a wide sweeping motion with his right hand at the words "went around the world" and made a burring noise in his throat like a large insect. He did this three times and again when *so?od* whirls around. I tried to get something more but Santos shut up like a clam."

[3]Probably Santos used this Kawaiisu word to indicate that his account was finished. However, I do not recognize the word.

[4]Possibly we have here a clue to the enigmatic nature of the tale.

noise again. Coyote went out and saw the little black thing on the ground. Coyote insisted on knowing what it was. The thing said it didn't have any mother or father or any other relative. It was the juice of tobacco. It didn't come from anywhere. Coyote went back into the house and told them that it was the juice of tobacco. They said that they would use it for medicine because it didn't have any relatives.[5]

D.   CAPPANNARI[6] (EMMA WILLIAMS: SADIE WILLIAMS)

Coyote had a brush house. He heard a noise flying around. It was a little piece of *sood*[7] [tobacco] juice. The other people talked to it. They asked *sood*, who are you? Where did you come from? *Sood* didn't answer. Coyote went out and said, "Talk to me. I am the chief." *Sood* said, "I have no mother, no father. I just grew on this earth."

E.   CAPPANNARI (MARIE GIRADO: CLARA GIRADO)

The old-timers saw a cake of *sood* out in the road. They didn't know what it was. They all gathered around and considered what it might be. It talked. It said it had no father, no mother.[8]

---

[5]This paragraph is taken from my *Ethnobotanical Studies among California and Great Basin Shoshoneans* (1941:249).

[6]Cappannari captions both these versions "Origin of Tobacco" and for the first he adds "Fragment."

[7]There are two species of tobacco known to the Kawaiisu: *so?odɨ*, *Nicotiana bigelovii*, and *ko?opi*, *N. attenuata*. However, *so?odɨ* was the preferred type and is always implied whenever reference is made to 'tobacco'.

[8]Cappannari has this comment: "Marie Girado explained that the people referred to above were "real" people, i.e., not in the mythological era of Coyote."

63. The Story of Pog^witɨ[1]

A.

ZIGMOND (EMMA WILLIAMS)

There was a bad man who lived at Old Town.[2] His name was pog^witɨ (geepɨ).[3] He was a murderer. He came down the trail which leads to Indian Creek along Hog Creek and is named Nettles Place (k^wiči?atabɨzi). He came to Walzer's place near Walker Basin. The people there gave him something to eat. Pog^witɨ asked where a certain man was. The man's wife said he was tanning a hide at a spring in keevinagihuyuwagadɨ[4] [a canyon apparently north of Walzer's]. Pog^witɨ went up there and stopped behind the man who was tanning. He talked to the man awhile and the other fellow kept on working. He didn't turn around. Pog^witɨ had an old-fashioned gun which was loaded with a ramrod. Pog^witɨ lifted his gun and shot the man through the back of the head. Then he ran away. People saw him running and sent some children to see what had happened. They found the man dead. Pog^witɨ went back to Old Town.

A man went to Kelso Valley to tell the dead man's relatives. His aunt started right away and walked all night to Walzer's. She wanted to burn the dead man right where he had died. She made a trench about two feet deep and put brush in it. Then she put the man's tule mat over the brush and the man on top of it. She put beads around his neck. She put in everything he had--baskets, arrows, etc. Then she burned him. That was the next morning. His pitacakavɨrawi [apparently pelvic bone] and his heart didn't burn at first.

---

[1]There is nothing in this story which could not have happened. It is an account of a "bad man" who is called pog^witɨ--Grizzly Bear--and who goes about killing people for no apparent reason. The several localities involved in his exploits are identified. It is not suggested that his name was acquired by reason of his murderous activities. However, the name presents problems. The grizzly bear itself is a symbol of evil and malice; "bear-impersonators" were known to exist; and the word pog^witɨ was apparently a synonym for tuhugadɨ (murderer or enemy--see Zigmond 1977:81). Under the circumstances, I shall simply tell the story the way it was told to me.

[2]Old Town was a village west of Tehachapi. It was later abandoned.

[3]The suffix -geepɨ means 'deceased' or 'discarded'.

[4]Literally, 'canyon against a mountain'.

(It takes a long time to burn them.) After everything was burnt, she covered up the place with dirt.

Some people were living at a place called *togowavo?ovɨzi* [Rattlesnake Spring] just northwest of Piute Ranch. The man and his wife had gone down into Sand Canyon to get pine-nuts. *Pog^w itɨ* came to the place where they lived at the spring. He asked an old lady, "Where are they?" She didn't know who he was. She said, "They went over there to get pine-nuts." He said, "I'm going over there to see them." It was in the early afternoon. As he walked, he passed over a hill and saw a deer which had been killed by a mountain lion. When he came to the man and woman, he said, "You people have lots of pine-nuts." He didn't sit down; he stood all the time. He told them about the deer he had seen. He said to the man, "Let's go get it." The two went to get the deer. They dragged it out of the shade. *Pog^w itɨ* didn't want to skin it; he waited for the man to do it. While the man was skinning the deer, *pog^w itɨ* was sitting on a rock above and behind him. *Pog^w itɨ* shot him in the back of the head.

Pog^w itɨ went back to the man's wife. He told her he had killed her husband. He wanted her to stay there in Sand Canyon with him all that night. The sun was going down. The woman left *pog^w itɨ* down there and came home. He followed her. When he came to the house, he went around it to the other side of the house. After that he came inside. The old woman told him to sit down. He slept there.

The next morning they went to bury the dead man. Many people went. *Pog^w itɨ* waited until they started. Then he followed and watched. They packed the man to a crack in the rocks in Sand Canyon. His wife was very busy. She put his beads around him. (On a man they put the beads around the neck and under one arm. On a woman they hang them like a necklace.) They began to cut up baskets to bury them, too. *Pog^w itɨ* was watching from a rock. "No, no," he said, "don't cut them up!" He wanted to get them later. They piled rocks on the body--big rocks so a coyote couldn't get to it. They burned his arrows later--maybe the next morning. *Pog^w itɨ* said, "I'm going home." After the people had gone off so that he couldn't see them any more, *pog^w itɨ* went back to where the body was. He threw all the rocks out and took off the blanket. He took the beads and everything that was inside. Then he cut open the body and removed the heart. He put just a few rocks back. [Emma didn't know what he did with the heart. She said, "Maybe he ate it."] He returned to Old Town. They found out later what he had done at the burial.

There was an old man who was living with his daughter in Oak Creek. *Pog^w itɨ* asked the daughter where the old man was. She said, "He's over there making fire." He was cutting up long logs with fire. (He used fire to cut the logs into pieces short enough to be used for kindling.) Then he packed them home. *Pog^w itɨ* said, "I can't stay long. I'll go over there and see him." He had a knife which he got from the Mexicans. [Apparently it was a curved metal knife.] He cut off the old man's arm at the shoulder, and stabbed him in the stomach. The old man died. He had no house--just a lean-to made of bark. The sun went down; the old man didn't come home. His daughter sent her two children after him. They found him and came back and said, "*Pog^w itɨ* killed him." The daughter and children went over there and stayed all night.

Next morning the daughter wrapped the old man in a blanket and

packed him home. She dug a hole all alone and buried him there. There were
no men around. She covered the body with dirt. Then she left for Kelso
Valley with her children. She was a good walker. She carried blankets,
acorns, and other things, and went from Oak Creek to some place on Indian
Creek by the time it was dark. Next day she reached a house she had in
Kelso Valley. She had gone with her father to Oak Creek to get some acorns.[5]

Some time later *pog^wit<del></del>* left Old Town with his two daughters, and
went to Kelso Valley. Some people saw him and said, "*Pog^wit<del></del>* is coming." He
stayed overnight with some people who lived down Cottonwood Creek at a place
called *soovip<del></del>zi*.[6] *Pog^wit<del></del>* told his daughters to go to see their mother whom
he had left long before. She lived at a place called *sigavarabi*, southwest
of St. John Mine. They left before sunrise. *Pog^wit<del></del>* didn't go with them.
He tried to kill the man in the house at Cottonwood Creek, but the man didn't
sleep so *pog^wit<del></del>* couldn't kill him.

The next day *pog^wit<del></del>* said to another man, "Let's go to South Fork."[7]
He said he would stay there two nights. The man took his blanket with him.
They came along the trail over the saddle that leads to John Weldon's place.
Pog^wit<del></del> was leading, but he told the man to go ahead. They came to a little
creek. As the man went over the creek, *pog^wit<del></del>* shot him with the old gun.
He hit him in the back and killed him. *Pog^wit<del></del>* kept on and went alone to
South Fork. He went to a spring there called *s<del></del>na?avivo?ov<del></del>zi* [Coyote Spring].[8]
He stayed there that night.

The next morning *pog^wit<del></del>* said to the brother of the man he had last
killed, "Let's go in the sweathouse (*t<del></del>vikahni*)." *Pog^wit<del></del>* had hidden his gun
in the *t<del></del>vikahni* before anyone saw. He said, "Let's get wood [to heat up the
t<del></del>vikahni]." They took off their clothes and took a sweatbath. *Pog^wit<del></del>* told
the man to go ahead of him into the water,[9] while he stayed in the sweathouse.
The man sat in the water and put water on his head. *Pog^wit<del></del>* took his gun and
shot him through the temple. Then he gathered up his clothes and ran off nude.
He didn't have time to dress.

Pog^wit<del></del> followed a trail up Scodie Mountain until he came to a
spring called *w<del></del>gab<del></del>*.[10] People lived there. *Pog^wit<del></del>* tried to kill a *kohoži*[11]
man there, but he didn't succeed.

---

[5]The Kawaiisu name for Oak Creek is *šiviid<del></del> huwipid<del></del>* (i.e., 'Valley-
Oak Canyon').

[6]*Soovip<del></del>* is 'cottonwood'.

[7]That is, the South Fork of the Kern River.

[8]Emma commented that she didn't know just where it is, but remembered
that Bob Rabbit's grandmother lived there.

[9]A sweathouse must be situated next to a pool since a dip (of whatever temperature) was essential after a sweatbath.

[10]*W<del></del>gab<del></del>* means 'vulva' or 'vagina'. Near the spring was a cracked
rock.

[11]*Kohoži* (or *kohoyži*) referred to people living in the nearby Panamint
region. They had frequent contact with the Kawaiisu.

People from South Fork[12] followed him up Scodie Mountain to kill him. It was night when *pogʷitɨ* reached there, so he went to sleep. The men who followed him came later. They went all around the house and sent one in to see if he was there. *Pogʷitɨ* was sleeping in a *tavikahni* [sunhouse], while an old man was sleeping in another. The men [who had come to kill *pogʷitɨ*] told the old man that in the morning he should go down to see *pogʷitɨ*, talk to him, and fool him. The old man went early the next morning and brought *pogʷitɨ* a basketful of shelled pinyons. The old man asked, "What's the matter, you still sleeping?" "Yes," said *pogʷitɨ*. He had tried to kill a *kohoži* man [see above] named *agapiši* who had slept near him.

The old man was sitting there. *Pogʷitɨ* was making a fire. The old man was waiting for the men to come to shoot *pogʷitɨ*. He wondered where they were. Then one of the men hiding behind the brush of the *tavikahni* put his rifle over the brush and shot *pogʷitɨ* in the chest. An old lady who was sleeping there was frightened by the shot. She jumped up nude.

The men came in, dragged *pogʷitɨ* out, shot him all over, and threw his body away. Then they went back to South Fork. Two of them came through Kelso Valley and this way [Piute] and said, "*Pogʷitɨ* can't come yet; he has a big load of pinyons." Then they told that he had been killed. They told *pogʷitɨ*'s two daughters.

Pogʷitɨ was mean. He would see somebody and kill him quick. Emma doesn't know if they buried him. They broke his gun. His daughters went to live with his mother at Old Town.

Emma's mother told her the story. She had seen him.

Emma commented: "Everybody treated *pogʷitɨ* right. He killed lots of people, but when he came into anyone's house they treated him right."

---

[12]South Fork was the principal area of the Tübatulabal, but these men are said to be Kawaiisu.

204

64. A Story of Cannibalism

A.   CAPPANNARI (EMMA WILLIAMS)

A Kawaiisu woman married an Indian who was apparently from Nevada. The woman lived north of Panamint.[1] The man probably spoke Koso.[2] The woman and her husband went to visit his mother. They had brush houses just like those of the Kawaiisu.

It was winter; there was snow. Her husband went with another man out one morning to hunt jackrabbits. Her husband killed that man and carried him home on his back. He left him outside the house and told his wife to "go after that wildcat outside." She found the corpse and did not bring him in. So her husband went out and got him. He put a pot on the fire, cut some meat off the man, and put it in the pot.

The dead man's wife lived in a brush house nearby, and she wanted some of the meat, too. The Kawaiisu woman was frightened. After dark she went out to get water. She left her jug at the spring and walked all that night and all the next day. It took her about three days to get back home above Panamint.

Emma commented: "Sometimes those people eat babies. A man sometimes eats his wife when she is having a baby. They hit her in the breasts with a stick. That kills her. They bake babies in the ground."[3] The people referred to speak a language "a little different from *kohoizua*."[4] They live in Nevada, north of Death Valley.

---

[1] This area would be to the northeast of the main Kawaiisu permanent dwelling region.

[2] Emma probably used the word *kohoži*.

[3] Cf. a version of the "Coyote Marries His Daughter" myth.

[4] Apparently plural of *kohoži*.

65. A Gambling Story[1]

A.

ZIGMOND (SETIMO GIRADO)

A Mexican boy was a shepherd. He played solitaire while watching the sheep. He talked to the cards: "Jack, you like me?" "Yes," said the jack. "The day after tomorrow I'm going to play cards at the saloon in the city," said the boy. "If you are at the bottom of the deck on each deal, no one can beat me." The card said, "Better look out for *inɨpi*. He's a good gambler. He has a mule to carry his money."

The boy went to town and played cards with the saloon keeper. Four jacks came up every time. The boy won all the money. The saloon keeper bet his saloon for $2,000. The saloon keeper dealt. The boy got four jacks and won. He kept the saloon and ran it.

The *inɨpi* said, "I'm going to play that boy." He had two mules loaded with money, and rode on a white horse. He went fast and got there the same evening. "Hello!" said the *inɨpi*. "Hello!" said the boy. The *inɨpi* said, "Let's play poker." The boy looked at the money on the mules. "All right," he said. They played. The boy dealt. They bet $1,000 and kept raising. The boy got four jacks; the *inɨpi* got three aces. The boy won all.

The boy wanted to get the gold cap worth $20,000 which the *inɨpi* had. They played for the cap. The *inɨpi* got four aces; the boy got four jacks. The *inɨpi* took everything. He asked the boy, "How much are you worth?" Apparently the boy said, "$1,000." The *inɨpi* said, "If I win, I'll take you with me. You'll get a good job." The *inɨpi* dealt and got four aces. The boy

---

[1]The setting of this story is clearly not Kawaiisu and not aboriginal. Most of the details seem to reflect the traditions and ways of life of non-Indians of pioneer days. The only "Kawaiisu" element is to be found in the supernatural character *inɨpi*, but even there Setimo often substituted the word 'devil'. To avoid confusion I have used *inɨpi* throughout. Actually, this 'devil' is not the typical Kawaiisu *inɨpi* (ghost, spirit), but the evil antagonist of Western religions.

The concepts associated with card-playing (though the Kawaiisu came to be acquainted with cards), cities, saloons, meal-time (announced by bell-ringing!), mules, riding equipment, the ocean (the Kawaiisu knew of it vaguely), whale, and other items are foreign to the native culture. One may assume a Mexican-American element in Setimo Girado's background.

got four jacks. The *inɨpi* said, "I get you. Be at my house when I ring the bell at noon for dinner tomorrow." The boy said, "All right." The *inɨpi* said, "There is a little lake there. My two daughters will be coming out of the water. You be there."

The boy kept looking for the water. It was getting late and he was afraid he wouldn't make it. He started running. Finally he saw the water, but could find no tracks. He hid in the brush by the lake. He saw two girls coming out of the water. He took the dresses and gave them to the girls. The older girl packed him on her back and flew a long way through the air. She dropped him near the house. The bell for lunch was ringing and the boy walked in. He ate with the *inɨpi*, his wife, and two daughters.

The *inɨpi* told the boy to sleep in the saddle-room in the barn. He said there were lots of blankets there. The boy looked in the barn. "I can't sleep there," he said. "I'm not a horse." The older daughter had a good house about thirty feet away from her father's house. The boy went to the daughter's house and knocked on the door. "Come in," she said. He slept with her. The girl told him he would be put to work digging out willows.

The boy started to work, but he said to himself, "It's too much; I'll never get finished." About ten in the morning his "wife" (the older daughter) came. He complained to her. She took a hoe and, with a few strokes, she cleared the field, ploughed, planted grain which started growing. At noon she packed the boy home. The lunch bell rang and they ate.

That night the wife told him that the next day he would be made to bring a pool of water to the house with pick and shovel. At breakfast the *inɨpi* told the boy what he had to do. The water was about ten miles away down a hill. The boy couldn't do the job. He threw down his shovel. His wife came at eleven. The boy complained. The wife took the shovel, made a few strokes, and the water went up the hill and down toward the house. The boy took the shovel as if he had done the job. At noon the *inɨpi* told him that he was a good boy and had done the job right.

At night his wife told him that the *inɨpi* had lost a gold ring in the ocean, and the boy must find it. She told him to take an axe with him. At breakfast the *inɨpi* said, "I lost a gold ring in the ocean. Find it by noon." The boy went to the ocean and looked around. He went into the water up to his neck, but couldn't go any farther. He came back to the shore and sat down. The wife came and he complained to her. She told him to take the axe and hit her over the head with the blunt edge. She had bread under her arms. At first he refused, but finally he did as she told him. She sank down into the water and swam under the water to the middle of the ocean. All the fish came around her, and she fed them pieces of bread. She told them to bring her the ring. A whale came but he didn't have the ring. The fish kept coming one after another, but without the ring. The last fish, a tiny one, far behind the others, came. He had the ring in his mouth. The wife swam back to the boy and gave him the ring. She packed him back to the house. The bell rang and the boy gave the ring to the *inɨpi*. The *inɨpi* was surprised that the boy had found the ring.

That night the wife said to the boy, "The *inɨpi* plans to kill you tomorrow. When he gives you a saddle and other equipment, don't take his.

Take mine." At breakfast the *inɨpi* said, "You are to ride four mules today. The saddle is in the corral." The boy went out, but he took his wife's equipment instead. The first mule kicked, but the boy roped and saddled him. Then the mule quieted down. The boy put blinders on him. The mule turned over. The boy jumped away. The mule kicked and bit, but the boy jumped on again. This was repeated until the mule was all worn out--nearly dead. The same thing happened with the second mule. As soon as the boy got the blinders on, the mule stopped fighting. And it was the same with the third mule. The fourth mule didn't buck at all. It was his wife turned into a mule. The other three were the *inɨpi*, his wife, and the other daughter. At noon they were all bloody from the beating the boy had given them. They washed themselves off and ate together.

That night the boy's wife said to him, "The *inɨpi* is going to kill you tomorrow. We're going away. We'll get on a horse together and ride to the big city. But don't look back." As they rode, the *inɨpi* came up from behind them, greeted them, and tried to make them look back. They didn't look back, and the *inɨpi* went home. He did this three times. At the third time, the boy looked back a little bit. He became crazy. His wife went on to town.

Kitanemuk Myths

66. Coyote Kidnaps Mountain Lion's Sons

A.   ZIGMOND (MARCELINO RIVERA AND ISABELLA GONZALES)

Mountain Lion lived a few miles from Tejon Rancheria[1] with his wife Jackrabbit, his twin sons, and his mother-in-law Gopher.[2] The people in that area didn't like Mountain Lion so they paid Coyote to kidnap his children.[3]

Coyote was living at Creek Canyon. He came up to Mountain Lion's mother-in-law who was taking care of the two little boys. Their father was out hunting. Their mother was gathering chia. Coyote told the old woman that he was thirsty and wanted a drink of water. He told her to bring the water in a sieve-like basket. She tried, but came back and said that she couldn't get any water in it. He replied that she could if she would plaster the bottom of the basket [apparently with mud]. She went away again, but when she returned, she found that Coyote was gone and had taken the children.

When Jackrabbit came home, Gopher told her what had happened. Then Mountain Lion came home and his wife told him that Coyote had stolen the boys. He was so angry that he picked up a burning brand and struck her on the back of the neck. It left a red spot which is still to be seen on jackrabbits. He asked his mother-in-law why she hadn't taken care of the children. He was about to hit her on the head with a rock, but she was sitting near a hole and so she dropped into it and the rock missed her.

Mountain Lion set out to look for Coyote and the boys, but Coyote had hidden them at his place in the canyon so they could not be found. As the boys grew bigger, they would go out and play. Coyote had children of his own, but they were not the same as Mountain Lion's sons. Coyote warned the boys not to go far. He was afraid that they might be found.

---

[1]This tale was told in the midst of the Tejon Rancheria, which in aboriginal days must have been a Kitanemuk center. The rancheria was absorbed in a great cattle ranch and the two narrators (brother and sister, I think) were the only Kitanemuk remaining.

[2]Though the sons are described as "twins," one was apparently bigger than the other.

[3]This reason for the kidnapping is not to be found in any of the Kawaiisu versions.

Mountain Lion kept looking all over the mountains and in the plain [the San Joaquin Valley], but he saw no trace of his sons. He had looked for them for twelve years. They were now big enough to go hunting by themselves. They would kill a deer and then tell Coyote. He would go after it.

As they grew older, the smaller son said to the larger son, "Don't you notice the difference between our hands and those of Coyote's other children? I don't believe he is our father." But the brother said that they were smaller than the other children and that was what made the difference.

Mountain Lion would go to the top of rocks to look around for his children. He couldn't eat and would cry a lot. He sang a song [but the narrators couldn't remember it].

Once the children went far off and killed a deer. The younger son kept thinking about Coyote not being their father. He said, "We can't be related to him. Look how big our hands are." They came across Mountain Lion's tracks. "Let's go up this way," the smaller one said. "We haven't been this way." He measured his hands against the tracks and found that they fitted exactly. They followed the tracks and heard someone talking. It was Mountain Lion talking to himself. They listened and heard him telling how Coyote had stolen his sons. Mountain Lion said that when he was young he could always see an arc shining around him "like the sun."[4] As he grew older he didn't see it any more. The smaller son had had the same experience. He said, "Let's go up and see him." The other boy didn't want to because he remembered that Coyote had said that there was a man around who would try to steal them and kill them. But the other brother said, "Let's go up anyway." And so they did.

They talked to Mountain Lion and he knew they were his children. The smaller one said, "Didn't I tell you that Coyote isn't our father? This one is our father." Mountain Lion kept some pinyons, juniper berries, and chia in his belt. He gave the boys some. After he had fed them, he said, "Coyote will smell the food and know what you ate. He will ask about it. You tell him that you were on the *tɨvaŋ* mountain where there are many pinyon trees and juniper bushes.[5]

When they got home, Coyote asked them right away about the smell of pinyon and juniper. They told him that they had been on the *tɨvaŋ* mountain where there were lots of them. They also told him about the deer they had killed. They wanted him to go after it. Coyote brought in the deer, but told them not to go so far away again. He said it was too far for him to carry the deer.

The next day the boys went hunting nearby and saw Mountain Lion again. They killed another deer, but Mountain Lion kept them until it would be too late for Coyote to come after it that night. It was lying under a mountain oak.[6]

---

[4]The presence of the "arc" is not explained.

[5]The name of the mountain is derived from *tɨva* 'pinyon'. The narrators explained that the name is also given to "five springs" which are located near the mountain.

[6]This oak tree was described as "not tall--with its branches spread out."

(When the boys were young, Mountain Lion had given them necklaces of gold and silver, but Coyote had taken them off and put them on his own children. In place of them, he had given Mountain Lion's sons necklaces of cane, oakwood, and rosebush wood.[7])

When the boys got home, they told Coyote that they had killed a deer. It was too late to go after it that night. "We'll show you where it is in the morning," they said. "All right," said Coyote. It was the habit of the boys to leave the deer carcass whole. Then Coyote would come and eat the guts and the rest of the "insides," and bring the carcass home.

In the morning the three started off together. Then the boys told Coyote to go ahead and they would catch up with him. They told him where the deer was. They took another way and arrived ahead of him. Coyote came to the deer under the oak tree. He noticed that the tree had a broken limb. He was suspicious and hesitated to go nearer. The boys assured him that it was all right. They said that they had played there and had broken the limb. Coyote came close but was reluctant to go inside the carcass. The boys urged him on. He cut a hole in the stomach and went in. He ate the heart, the liver, and the other internal organs.

The boys had told Mountain Lion that when Coyote was getting full and feeling good, he would wag his tail. He saw Coyote's tail wag. He quickly closed up the opening where Coyote had entered. There was a small hole in the deer's neck where the blood had been let out when it had been killed. Coyote looked out of the hole and saw Mountain Lion. He begged Mountain Lion not to kill him. "I worked hard and raised your sons," he said, "and now that they are grown up, you can have them." But Mountain Lion said, "You made me worry and suffer all these years, and so now I will have to kill you."

Mountain Lion killed him, and then went on to Coyote's house and killed his wife and children. Then Mountain Lion and his sons went to live on *tɨvaŋ* where there is lots of food.

---

[7]The gold and silver necklaces must have been a modern touch. The necklaces are usually described as made of beads--which also are valued as money. Coyote's necklaces are said to be made of sections of cane (*Phragmites australis*) which are hollow and could conveniently be used as "beads."

67. Coyote Marries His Daughter

A.   <u>ZIGMOND (MARCELINO RIVERA AND ISABELLA GONZALES)</u>

Coyote was living in his house, and he went out hunting. He thought of a way to have his daughter. When he came home, he acted as if he was hurt. He said that he had been attacked by a bear. His daughter came to help him home and packed him on her back. When they came near the house, she was angry because he was "playing" with her. She threw him down, ran home, and told her mother to go after him.

Coyote told his wife, Frog, to get some wood and burn him because he was very sick and was going to die. Before they burned him, he told his family to go to the other side of the mountain to his friend who looked just like him. He said that his daughter should marry his friend. Before they put him on the pile of wood, he told them not to look back as they went away or they would see his ghost. But, as they were running away, the little son looked back. He said he saw his father jump off the pile. His mother was angry and said that now they would all die.

Coyote ran around the mountain to the place where his "friend" was supposed to be. All the family was crying along the way because their father was dead. They came to the place. The wife was crying. Coyote asked her why she cried. She told him that his friend had died. He cried because he was glad. He shed big tears that made holes in the ground. He sang: "Salt-grass, drink, drink!" because he was so happy.[1] When she had stopped crying, the mother told the "friend" that Coyote had said that he should marry his daughter. The "friend" replied that he would do it because Coyote was his friend. He told the sun to go down so that night would come. He blew tobacco at the sun to make it go away. "Run, sun!" he said. He cried because he was glad.

He went hunting rats with his son. He called the boy "my son" instead of "my brother-in-law." "Oh, I forgot to call you brother-in-law!" he said. The boy told his mother that the "friend" had called him "son" instead of "brother-in-law."

The daughter was pregnant. Her mother was angry because she knew that the "friend" was really Coyote. She squeezed the fetuses out of her daughter. There were seven little coyotes. She gathered some wood and roasted

---

[1]The significance of this appeal to "salt-grass" is not clear.

them.

       Coyote was out hunting. When he returned, he saw the ashes. He poked through them with a stick. He saw the roasted coyotes and thought they were rats. He ate them. Then he went to drink water.

       The family had gone up into the sky. Coyote saw a reflection of them in the water. His wife and children were laughing at him. He tried to reach them in the water. He called to them to come down and eat the rats. But the family stayed in the sky and formed a star-cluster of seven stars [apparently the Pleiades]. These are the mother, the son, four daughters, and the mother's hat. There is another cluster of three stars--Coyote, his bow, and arrow. The two groups are not close to one another because Coyote never reached his family.

Panamint Myths

68. The Theft of Fire[1]

A.   <u>ZIGMOND (PANAMINT GEORGE: ANDY SHOSHONE)</u>

Coyote had a large family. There was nothing to do and no fire.
Coyote said he was going to get fire.

He told the family to get two sticks, and he made two balls of deerskin. He planted the sticks at a distance [?]. Two people run and get the
sticks and then run back and throw them. They throw the balls at the sticks
and make one point for each stick hit, but no points if the ball touches both
sticks. The ball touched both sticks.

Coyote made eight sticks of split cane about a foot long. They
were painted red on the inside and white on the outside. A person throws them
at his knee and they bounce off.

They played the hand game. A man holds a white stick and a black
stick--one in each hand. He puts his hands behind him, sings, brings his
hands in front and folds his arms. The other player must guess where the white
one is.

One player shoots an arrow and the others try to hit it. If an arrow lies over the target-arrow, it counts two points. An arrow lying closest
but not touching the target-arrow counts one point.

They had another game. The women sell food and the men must buy.
If the women have nothing to sell they must go out hunting.

Lizard wasn't doing anything. He was sleeping in the sun on a rock.
As he was lying there, something black came slowly from the sky and fell close
by him. He told the people to come to see it and to find out what it was.
Everyone came to look at the black thing. Coyote knew what it was. He said
it was a coal of fire. Something was burning somewhere. There was fire

---

[1]The two Panamint myths, "The Theft of Fire" and "The Theft of Pinyons," were told to me in 1937 by Panamint George and Johnnie Shoshone, respectively. They share a common characteristic. Both are introduced with a
brief and incomplete account of the playing of games and gambling. These
initial descriptions seem to have little or no connection with the tales which
follow.

somewhere. Coyote said, "Everyone must jump to see where it is." The first
one jumped a little way. Everyone tried but couldn't jump high enough. It
was Coyote's turn. "I'm going to beat all of you. Watch me." He jumped
just a little way--not as much as the others.

There was one left: Hummingbird. All the others said, "He can't
do anything; he's too fast." "Watch me!" said Hummingbird. He got ready. He
jumped high in the air. Coyote was the first to lose sight of him. One by
one they lost sight of him. Finally only Lizard lying on the rock could see
him. He told the others where Hummingbird was. Lizard watched him until he
was high up on the branch of a big tree. Hummingbird stopped there. He looked
north, then he looked east, then south, then west. He kept looking over there
toward the west. Lizard was telling the people what he was doing. "He's coming down now," Lizard said. People one by one caught sight of him as he came
down. Coyote was the last to see him. He landed in the midst of the people.

Coyote asked Hummingbird, "What did you see up there?" "I saw
nothing toward the north, nothing toward the east, nothing toward the south.
I saw fire toward the west. There were a lot of people around--and a big fire
in the center." Coyote said, "That's our fire. Someone has to go after it."
Coyote said he was going after it with his family. The fastest one was put at
the back--farthest from the fire. The slowest was near the fire. Coyote put
Turtle nearest the fire--he was the slowest.

Coyote had a string bound around his head about a foot high and put
red paint on his face. He wanted to disguise himself. People [guarding the
fire] were doing war dances around the fire. He joined in the dancing; they
didn't know him. He danced, crying: "*či-he-he ci-he-he*!" Someone said,
"That's Coyote!" Coyote said, "Yes, that's Coyote!" Someone said, "Throw him
in the fire!" Coyote said, "Throw him in the fire!" They took him and threw
him in the fire. He jumped 'way to the other side. He started dancing on the
other side. They said, "Shoot him with two war-arrows!" One shot at him. He
jumped aside. Another shot at him. He jumped aside.

Coyote got angry. He pushed his string-covered head into the fire.
It caught fire. Then he started running. When he ran, the fire went out.
Women said, "What's he trying to do with his hair?" He tried again and again,
but each time the fire went out.

There was a big pond over there. It had no bottom to it. "Throw
him in there," they said. Coyote said, "Yes, throw him in there!" They caught
him and threw him in. He jumped 'way to the other side. He kept on dancing
all night. And he kept trying to catch the fire. At last he was able to
carry the fire a little farther, and it burned well on his head. The big fire
was burning low. Coyote was going fast. "Kill him!" they said.

They caught Coyote just as he reached Turtle. They killed him.
Turtle ran on until he came to Lizard, and then they killed him. Lizard ran on
to another Lizard [another kind] and then they killed him. The second Lizard
ran to a bird and then was killed. The bird threw the fire to another bird.
Each one was killed when he was caught. The last one was Jackrabbit. The
bird gave the fire to him. They were chasing Jackrabbit. It started raining
big drops. He cried, "k^wa, k^wa!" He put the fire under his tail. That's why
it's still black there. He cried again, "k^wa, k^wa!"

222

Rat lives up on a rock. He heard the cry and came down. They were about to catch Jackrabbit. Rat caught the Fire. He zigzagged first one way and then another. He came to the rock and they thought they had him. He went up to his house in the rock. In a little while, smoke started coming out of his house.

People below were freezing. Everything was burning above. They told Rat to throw down some fire. He would come out and throw a little bit down. He kept doing that to tease them. Pretty soon he threw fire everywhere. "Everybody is going to have fire everywhere," Rat said. He kicked it all around.

That's why there's fire everywhere now.

69.   The Theft of Pinyons

A.

ZIGMOND (JOHNNIE SHOSHONE: ANDY SHOSHONE)

There were many people around Furnace Creek in Death Valley. They were playing the stick game--eight sticks are bounced off the knee [see "The Theft of Fire"]. Crow was sitting over on one side; he wasn't playing. He "coughed up" and a pinyon nut came out. He didn't know what it was. He went over and showed it to the people. Coyote knew what it was. "This is a pinyon nut," he said. "It comes from the north. We'll go get some."

Everyone went over there to gamble with those people and win the pinyons. They came to a place where pinyon trees were all around. The other people went to the other side [?]. Coyote went by himself.

People were making pinyon mush, but under it was excrement--just to tease Coyote. He ate a little, but didn't like it. He put it down. There was a woman walking around there. He tried to copulate with her but she didn't like him. He went back to the others. They were gambling with the hand [guessing] game [see "The Theft of Fire"]. They had pinyon mush in basket dishes. They told him to eat some. "It's just the same over there where I was," he said, but he tasted it. "It's pinyon mush," he said. He ate it all night while the others were gambling.

In the morning they were playing hit-the-arrow game [see "The Theft of Fire"]. Coyote said, "I'm going to play that." Two Owls were to be his opponents. They were of the pinyon people. Coyote's people had won much from the other people when they played all night. They gave everything to Coyote to bet. But he lost it all to the opposite side. Finally he bet himself and his people. Everyone would be killed if he lost.

Coyote cried to his people, "Don't think of me." He thought he would lose. Crow said he would help him. Coyote and the two Owls shot their arrows, but none of them hit. Crow had one arrow left. "I'm going to urinate," he said. He took his arrow with him, and split it a little at the point. Coyote went over and stood near the target-arrow. "It's right here," he said. Crow shot, hit the target-arrow right at the end near the feathers, and pushed it over to the other arrows on the side.[1]

---

[1]The situation is not clear to me. Apparently the split arrow caught the target-arrow in the split and dragged it to a favorable spot in

Crow kept winning. He won everything back--everything the pinyon people had. They had nothing more to bet. Coyote said, "Why don't you bet your pinyons?" "All right," they said. They bet the pinyons. Coyote's people won.

But the losers didn't want to give up their pinyons. "We eat them," they said. They gathered them in a basket and put it high up in a pine tree. As they came down, they cut the branches so that no one could climb up. Lots of their people stayed around the tree. Rattlesnake, Bear--all the mean ones-- stayed next to the tree, and the others were all around, so that no one could get to the tree. They slept there.

Coyote was discussing with his people how they were going to get the pinyons down. "What are we going to do?" he asked. "You ought to know," they said. "Yes, I know," said Coyote. They talked about it all night. At dawn he told Woodpecker to cut a piece of deerskin in half. Woodpecker put the pieces over his own head and down to his mouth. You can still see the marks on his head; his long tongue is the lower part of the skin. Another Woodpecker (a smaller kind) put a thorn of a cactus on the bottom of each of his feet (like stilts). He walked on the thorns between the sleeping people. The big Woodpecker walked on his three toes. The people slept; they didn't wake up. The Woodpeckers reached the tree. They climbed up--the big one first. When he got near the pinyons, he stuck out his long tongue and got two pinyons from the basket. Then they came down the tree, passed over the people, and reached their own people. "Let's get home," they said.

They talked over the matter of who would carry the pinyons. Coyote said, "The fastest runner will be at the end." Coyote was to be the first to carry the pinyons. One pinyon was bad. "Coyote will eat the pinyon when he runs," they said. They gave him the bad one. He started off. When he got far away, he put it in his mouth and tried to eat it. There was nothing in it. "We knew he would do that," they said as they watched him. They began to run with the good pinyon. The slowest one started.

It was nearly noon. The pinyon people woke up. They looked in the basket and saw that the pinyons were missing. "Let's chase them," they said. They started running. Just as they caught up with the one who had the pinyon, he would pass it to another. They killed the one who had carried the pinyon, but by that time it was being carried by someone else. They kept running in relay. They got near Scotty's Castle in Grapevine Canyon [at the north end of Death Valley]. There were only five carriers left, all birds, the fastest and meanest. One was killed there at Scotty's Castle, another at Surveyors Well, another at Salt Creek. There were two left: Crow and a bird called *tuguvoyoči*. One of the pursuers knew where the pinyon was. He told the others. Crow tried to hide it under his tongue, but the one pursuer knew.

They were coming past Furnace Creek. "Don't kill them; get them alive!" the pursuers said. Crow didn't know where to hide the pinyon. He put it under the toes of one leg which then became rotten. They caught him by the rotten leg. They hit him with the leg and threw it far away. They killed *tuguvoyoči*, and he can still be seen about five miles south of Furnace Creek

---

relation to the other arrows.

(the formation is now called Mushroom Rock). The pursuers sat down and smoked. "Let's take a rest before we look for the pinyon," they said. They thought it was still on Crow. They looked all over him, inside and out. They couldn't find it. They pulled off his feathers. It was nowhere to be found. "Maybe it's on that leg," they said. But they could find only its tracks. It had run away.

They looked up. Pinyon trees were growing on the mountains. Fires were burning. People were cooking the pinyons. Crow was flying above with a pinyon in his mouth. The pinyon people said, "Throw that nut down so that we can take it back." Crow dropped it and then swooped down and caught it before it hit the ground.

Some of those people stayed here--Chipmunk, Bluebird--all the animals around here who eat pinyons. Woodpecker and Goose [he apparently was the one who told where Crow was hiding the pinyon nut] went back. Lots of them went back. All the pinyon trees are dead up there now. There are no pinyons up there.

70. Coyote and his Brother Wolf

A.   ZIGMOND (PANAMINT GEORGE: ANDY SHOSHONE)

There were two brothers. Wolf was the elder and Coyote the younger.
Coyote had big breasts; he looked like a woman. Wolf went hunting and killed
deer. Coyote gathered seeds.

The elder brother went hunting one day and came back with nothing.
That evening he lay down in his house and wouldn't eat. Coyote offered him
food, but he wouldn't take any. He started off again the next morning, but
came back with nothing. Again he lay down in the house and wouldn't eat.

The next morning Coyote talked to his brother but the latter didn't
move. Wolf said that something frightens him when he hunts deer--something
with a big knife comes along as he skins the deer and makes him run away.
Coyote said he would go with him to see. He took off his breasts and put on
shoes. They started off. Wolf sang a song as they walked along. Coyote tried
to sing with him but didn't get the tune right.

They went up a mountain, and came to deer tracks. Coyote said it was
a big track; Wolf said it is a little one. (Coyote talked a little different
from his brother.) They came to another track. Coyote said it was big.
They followed it a distance. A deer jumped out of the brush and ran up the
trail. Coyote started right after it running fast. Wolf followed slowly.
Coyote went over the mountain. Wolf came up slowly and found his brother
sitting down. Blood was coming out of Coyote's mouth. Wolf passed him by;
Coyote told him to go on. Wolf went over the mountain chasing the deer.
Finally he overtook the deer and got in front of it. He kept watching it and
waited for Coyote. He waited a long time. When Coyote came, he asked, "Did
you get him already?" "He's standing right there," said Wolf. He told Coyote
to shoot it. Coyote shot, but the arrow didn't go in far. Wolf shot, and
the deer fell down dead.

Coyote went up to the deer, dragged it over, and started to skin it.
Wolf got ready to run. He was afraid. Soon they heard someone singing:
$n\pm k^w amatu$ $n\pm k^w amatu$ $matutk^w i$ $wi\check{c}ika.$[1] They could see a knife swinging in the
brush. Wolf started to run. Coyote stayed and kept on with the skinning.

---

[1]No meaning was given to the words, but it may be noted that the
name (see below) seems to be involved.

The singing continued. At last a man came out swinging his knife. He cut rocks, and cut down pine trees. As he sang, he came toward the deer. Coyote was cutting up the deer. He wasn't frightened. The man was coming over the mountain cutting everything. He came close to the deer, took hold of it and tried to drag it away. Coyote pulled it back. Coyote was angry. He jumped on the man and started wrestling with him. He got the man down, took his knife, and cut his head off. He threw the head away. Wolf came back. He said, "You should have told me long ago that you would come with me and kill him."

Coyote finished with the deer. He told his brother to take it home. He said he was going to track the man he had killed. He wanted to find out where he came from. He followed the tracks into the middle of a pine forest. The man's wife, children, and the grandmother were living there. Coyote asked, "Where is your father?" "He went over there to frighten Wolf," they said. "Then he gets the deer and brings it here. He'll be back soon." Coyote asked the smallest child his name. "Nɨk^{w}ama," he said. Then he asked the next child. He said, "nɨk^{w}ama." Everyone in the family had the same name. The mother, grandmother, and father were all named nɨk^{w}ama.[2]

Coyote got angry. He took a stick and killed every member of the family. He went inside the house. There was a door. He broke it down. He came to another door. He broke it down. There he found all the deer skins the man had taken from Wolf--as well as meat. Coyote packed it all on his back and took it home.

-----

[2]The name given here is apparently included in the "man's" song as transcribed above. Marie Girado, one of the Kawaiisu narrators of myths, gives two names of fearful giants. One is *haakapainiži*, which is also mentioned by Emma Williams, another story teller. The other is *nɨkama*, mentioned only by Marie. While in this Panamint tale *nɨk^{w}ama* is not described as a giant, it will be noticed that he cuts through "everything"--rocks and trees. Since the Kawaiisu and the Panamint lived in close proximity, there may have been an exchange of stories and of mythological characters.

71. The Race to Koso Hot Springs

A.   ZIGMOND (PANAMINT GEORGE: ANDY SHOSHONE)

The animals were gathering carizzo grass [cane, *Phragmites australis*]
in the area around Barstow and Victorville so that they could eat the sugar on
it. Coyote said, "Let's race to Koso Hot Springs," That's where they lived.
He thought he could win.

They started. Coyote was ahead, but he tired near Randsburg. The
other animals passed him. Then he went faster. He passed Turtle, then Frog.
They were under the creosote bush [*Larrea tridentata*]. Coyote threw dirt on
them as he passed. He saw the other animals just this side of the Hot Springs.
But Coyote felt water on himself. He looked up and saw Frog jumping over him
and urinating on him. Frog passed the others and was ahead. Coyote came up
to Bear and pulled him along as he went. Bear was so heavy as he moved along
the canyon that Coyote was on his knees. Frog won.

A fire had been made at the end of the race at the Hot Springs, and
a pot of water was on the fire. The losers were to be thrown in. Coyote was
to push Sun in. Sun was this side of the pot [?]. All the people went in the
winterhouse. Coyote looked around to see which way he was going to run after
he would push Sun in and it got dark. Then he threw Sun in the water in the
pot. After that he ran a little, but it got dark and he couldn't see anything.
He began to crawl around. He was calling the people, but they didn't answer.
They didn't like him. He crawled over mountains. He fell down and rolled
over. Finally the others called him. He came over. They told him where the
entrance to the winterhouse was. He came inside and crawled around until he
came upon his brother-in-law, Owl. "Why didn't you call to me?" Coyote asked
him.

Coyote lay down in a corner. He was thin and hungry. He heard
people eating. "Why don't you give me something to eat?" he asked. Rat, Mouse,
and Owl came over and held food to his nose. Then they gave him something to
eat and went out to get some more. They went a little way out of the house
and brought more food back.

People asked Coyote if it was going to stay dark all the time. He
told them that they would have to cry out. He called them one by one. First
was Woodpecker. When he cried, the dawn came. Next was Crow. When he cried,
it went dark again. Then *kuraviya* (a duck with a long neck) cried and it became a little lighter. Coyote said, "I'm going to cry now." He cried and

231

everything went dark again. Coyote told Willow Woodpecker to cry. He did
and the Sun came up.

Everyone came out of the house. Coyote came out. Everything was
green. Coyote went over there and ate. "It tastes good," he said. He went
over and lay in the sun. Then he ate some more; it was sweet. "I'm going to
make everything sweeter." He urinated on everything. He told the people to
taste it now. They tasted everything, but it was no good. It was hot "like
chili." He spoiled it. They told him he was good for nothing. He spoiled
everything. That's how everything tastes now.

72.   Cottontail and the Sun

A.

ZIGMOND (PANAMINT GEORGE: ANDY SHOSHONE)

Cottontail slept all the time in the water. It was hot. Sun would pass low over him in the sky. He would reach to Cottontail's back with a stick and count his vertebrae: "One, two, three, four, five, six, seven, eight." Sun kept doing this all the time.

Cottontail got angry. In the morning before Sun came up, Cottontail's mother gave him some red seeds (*poiya*) to take with him when he went to the spring. He had a pile of them. He put a rock over it so that his mother wouldn't eat any. He went up to the mountain where Sun would come out. He hid so that he could shoot Sun when it came up. While he waited, Sun rose far below. Next morning Cottontail went to that place (where Sun had come up) and hid. This time Sun rose in another place. Sun kept doing that.

A tree stood by the water. When Sun would come up out of the water, it would bounce on the tree to dry off. Then it would go on.

Cottontail asked all the bushes how they burn. They all said that they burn roots and all. Only one bush was left. "How do you burn?" asked Cottontail. "When I burn, only my leaves burn," said the bush.[1] .Cottontail dug under this bush. He dug a hole which turned back over itself under the bush.

Sun came up and stopped at the tree at the edge of the water to dry off. Cottontail shot an arrow at Sun. The arrow burned up. He shot all his arrows. They all burned up. Then he decided to shoot with a fire-drill.[2] He shot and knocked Sun down to the edge of the water. Where Sun fell, all the ground got hot. Cottontail went underneath into his house. When the bush burned, only the leaves burned. Sun's heat went into the hole, but Cottontail kept going into the place where the hole turned back on itself.

---

[1]In the Chemehuevi tale which Laird calls "How Cottontail Rabbit Conquered the Sun" (1976:152-4), Cottontail similarly finds a bush under which he takes shelter from the fire of the sun.

[2]Obviously the fire-drill was regarded as more fire-resistant than arrows. As described, the former consisted of a cane (*Phragmites australis*) mainshaft and a sagebrush (*Artemisia tridentata*) foreshaft.

233

Cottontail's neck is brown where the heat struck him.

Cottontail took pieces of the sinew of mountain sheep. He threw one on the ground. It burned up. One after another all the pieces burned as he threw them on the ground. He had one left. He threw that one; it didn't burn. He felt the ground with his hand. It was cool. He came out. Sun was lying dead. He looked at it and wondered what he could make a new sun of. He cut a little ball out of Sun's heart and put it in the sky. He said it would be Sun. He took out the kidney and put it in the sky. He said that would be the moon following the sun.

Cottontail started home. As he went along, he saw many large Squirrels. A Squirrel said, "Look at that Cottontail. He killed Sun." Cottontail got angry. "I'll kill all of you," he said. "You can't kill us because we have a house under the rock," they said. Cottontail came toward them. They went under the rock. Cottontail came over and sat down. He said, "*yuwarambi buutat*,"[3] and blew hard. The rock broke into pieces and flew away. There were the Squirrels sitting down. Cottontail took a stick and killed them all.

Cottontail was walking along and came to a house. A lot of children were playing around there. Cottontail asked where the parents were. "They are gathering *poiya* (red seeds)," the children said. There was much of it around there. Cottontail told the children to make a fire. They did. Cottontail took hot stones and parched the seeds in a basket.[4] After parching a lot of them, he ground them. Then he made a mush of them. He told the children to get plates, and he gave all of them mush to eat. They became very full. Cottontail said, "Let's play." They played. Cottontail climbed a juniper tree and bent it over. He told them all to get on the end. It was like a see-saw. They all played and laughed. Then he let go of the tree. It sprang back and all of them were killed.

Cottontail started off again and came to another place. There was a lot of ripe *poiya* there. He cut it off with his teeth. He was sitting in the brush on the side. He was waiting for people who were coming to gather the seeds. They saw that the *poiya* was all cut off. "Cottontail has been doing that," they said. "He may be around here. Let's kill him." They looked all over, but they couldn't find him. Then he jumped up and ran. They chased him. He went under a rock. They started digging. They could see him, but he wasn't there. He blew a hole right through and ran on.

He came to a woman who was working on a basket waterbottle. She was an old woman. Cottontail went inside the basket. She was turning it around. It was heavy with Cottontail in it. "What's making it heavy?" she said. She looked inside and saw Cottontail. "When did you get in there?" she asked. Cottontail came out. "Why don't you get in there?" he asked. "It's fun watching you work from the inside." The woman got in. Cottontail worked on

---

[3]The transcription is only approximate. No meaning was given.

[4]A common procedure for preparing seeds and similar items as food is to shuffle them rapidly with hot coals in a winnowing basket. Hot stones could serve the same purpose. The seeds were then ground and cooked to mush.

234

the basket. He worked fast. He closed the opening so that she couldn't get out. He pushed the basket out and rolled it down the hill. The old woman was killed.

Cottontail went on. He came to a woman who was winnowing beaver-tail cactus [*Opuntia* sp., *navumbɨ*]. He was standing where the thorns were flying.[5] "What are you doing there?" she asked him. "The thorns will get in your eyes." "It's fun," he said, and kept playing around there. He told the woman to stand where he was. She did. He winnowed. She opened her eyes wide. The thorns went in her eyes and killed her.

Cottontail went on and came to a house. Smoke was coming out of it. Two women were playing a game. He sat down and watched them. They kept playing a long time. They moved around. "Why are you doing that?" he asked. "We've been playing a long time," they said. He looked up and saw a big rock hanging on the wall. He was sitting under it. The women got up and went out. They pulled a rope that let the rock fall on Cottontail. They could hear Cottontail crying. They thought they had killed him. They peeked in. He had jumped out of the way and was sitting in a corner. He told them to come in and to hang the rock up again. "Play that game again," he said. They played a little while. He started moving around. "Why are you moving around?" they asked. "I'm getting tired," he said. Then he stood up and went out. He pulled the rope. The rock fell down. He peeked in and saw that they were killed. He went away.

Cottontail walked along and came to another house with smoke coming out of it. He went inside. The woman said to him, "Sit over there on that little skin." But he sat by the door and put paint all over his face. The woman's sister came running in. She was frightened when she saw him and ran out. Others kept coming in, were frightened, and ran out again. It was cold and snowing. The woman told Cottontail to take the paint off. "My sister might freeze out there," she said. He took the paint off. Then they all came in and sat by him. They told him to move over. He moved over. They kept coming. He had to move over until he was sitting on the woman's leg.

They all went to sleep. Cottontail went outside and got a long log. It was so long it extended through the house to the other side. He started it burning in the middle of the house. He made a hole through the log by blowing. Then he went to sleep inside it. The log was on fire. He sang with a flute and kept them all sleeping. Then he tied all of them to one another. He lay down. The house started burning. Cottontail yelled, "Fire!" He pulled the woman out, but the others couldn't get out. "Let go of me!" they yelled to each other. They all burned to ashes.

Cottontail and the woman went away. Then they stopped and talked. Cottontail told the woman to shut her eyes while he hid. He ran under a rock. She looked for him and saw him under the rock. She thought she had him, but he went right through. She made a big fire around the rock. She could hear him coughing underneath. She thought she had killed him, but he came around

---

[5]The woman was cleaning the thorns off the cactus fruit so that it could be eaten.

from the other side. Then he told her to do the same thing. He closed his eyes while she hid under the rock. He made a fire around the rock and she was burned up.

He went along and came to Mountain Sheep. "Look! That's Cottontail," they said. "He killed the Sun!" "I'll kill you," said Cottontail. He was angry. "You can't kill us," they said. "You can't climb where we go." They climbed up the rocks. He sat down and watched them. He told them he had good medicine; it smelled good. It came from the east. They wanted to smell it. "Throw it up here!" they said. He threw it up. They liked the smell. All of them smelled it. "Throw it down when you've finished," said Cottontail. They threw it down, but all of them fell down with it. It was a steep precipice, and all of them were killed.

Cottontail walked along. He came to his own home. His mother said, "There's a big rock on top of your food. It's so big I can't move it." Cottontail went over to it, picked it up, and tossed it away. Then he brought the seed to his mother.

References

Aldrich, J. M.
   1912   The Biology of Some Western Species of the Dipterous Genus Ephydra. *Journal of the New York Entomological Society* 20:77-99.

Barrett, Samuel A.
   1919   Myths of the Southern Sierra Miwok. *University of California Publications in American Archaeology and Ethnology* 16:1-28.

Benedict, Ruth
   1926   Serrano Tales. *Journal of American Folklore* 39:1-17.

Blackburn, Thomas C.
   1975   *December's Child: A Book of Chumash Oral Narratives.* University of California Press.

Booth, Curtis, and Maurice L. Zigmond
   n.d.   *The Kawaiisu Language (Part 2: Kawaiisu Dictionary).* Ms.

Cappannari, Stephen C.
   1947- *Kawaiisu Fieldnotes.* Ms.
   1949

Gayton, Anna H.
   1935   Areal Affiliations of California Folktales. *American Anthropologist* 37:582-99.

Gayton, Anna H., and Stanley S. Newman
   1940   Yokuts and Western Mono Myths. *University of California Anthropological Records* 5:1-109.

Gifford, Edward W.
   1923   Western Mono Myths. *Journal of American Folklore* 36:302-67.

Harrington, John P.
   1969   *Chemehuevi Noun List.* (Edited by Kenneth C. Hill). Mimeographed.

Kelly, Isabel T.
   1932   Ethnography of the Surprise Valley Paiute. *University of California Publications in American Archaeology and Ethnology* 31: 67-210.

Kroeber, Alfred L.
1907   Indian Myths of South Central California. *University of California Publications in American Archaeology and Ethnology* 4: 167-250.

Laird, Carobeth
1974   The Buffalo in Chemehuevi Folklore. *Journal of California Anthropology* 1:220-4.

1976   *The Chemehuevis*. Banning, California: Malki Museum Press.

1977a   Intimations of Unity. *Journal of California Anthropology* 4: 50-54.

1977b   Chemehuevi Myth as Social Commentary. *Journal of California Anthropology* 4:191-5.

Lowie, Robert H.
1924   Shoshonean Tales. *Journal of American Folklore* 37:1-242.

McCown, Theodore D.
1929   *Kawaiisu Fieldnotes*. Ms.

Sapir, Edward
1930   The Southern Paiute Language. *Proceedings of the American Academy of Arts and Sciences* 65:1-730.

Schmerler, Henrietta
1931   Trickster Marries His Daughter. *Journal of American Folklore* 44: 196-207.

Steward, Julian H.
1936   Myths of the Owens Valley Paiute. *University of California Publications in American Archaeology and Ethnology* 34:355-440.

Thompson, Stith
1929   *Tales of the North American Indians*. Bloomington: Indiana University Press.

Twisselmann, Ernest C.
1967   A Flora of Kern County, California. *Wasmann Journal of Biology* 25: 1-395.

Voegelin, Charles F.
1935   Tübatulabal Texts. *University of California Publications in American Archaeology and Ethnology* 34:191-246.

Voegelin, Erminie W.
1938   Tübatulabal Ethnography. *University of California Anthropological Records* 2:1-90.

Walker, Ardis M.
1971   *The Rough and the Righteous of the Kern River Diggins*. Balboa Island, California: Paisano Press

Zigmond, Maurice L.

1941   *Ethnobotanical Studies among California and Great Basin
        Shoshoneans*. Linotyped, Ann Arbor, Michigan, 1971.

1977   The Supernatural World of the Kawaiisu. In *Flowers of the Wind*,
        Thomas C. Blackburn, Ed. Socorro, New Mexico: Ballena Press.

1979   Kawaiisu Basketry. *Journal of California Anthropology* 5:199-215.

n.d.   *Kawaiisu Ethnobotany*. To be published by the University of Utah
        Press.

Explanation of Figures

1a. (l.-r.) Gladys Nichols, her mother Lizzie Nichols, her sister Emma Williams, Emma's daughter Sophie Williams, and Sophie's daughter Elsie Williams, 1936. Elsie married Jess Garcia, a Spanish-American, the following year.

b. Emma Williams with Maurice Zigmond, with Emma's house in background, 1936. Emma was Zigmond's primary Kawaiisu consultant (1936-1940); she also worked with McCown (in 1929) and with Cappannari (in 1947-1949).

2a. Sadie Williams, another of Emma Williams' daughters, 1937. She translated her mother's narratives for Cappannari.

b. Sophie Williams and other Kawaiisu women pruning wild tobacco (*Nicotiana bigelovii*), 1937.

3a. John Nichols, husband of Lizzie Nichols, with his left hand in a mortar-hole, 1937. John was a consultant for both McCown and Zigmond.

b. John and Louisa Marcus in front of their house at Monolith, 1937. John was an important consultant for Zigmond; Louisa told Zigmond one myth.

4a. Refugia Williams and her two daughters in Bakersfield, 1937. Refugia was perhaps the best-known Kawaiisu woman, but was quite old and feeble when Zigmond met her; she died in 1938.

b. Sam Willie and his family, 1937. They lived in Monolith near John Marcus. John and Sam took Zigmond to some pictograph and mortar-hole sites. The young lady in the doorway is probably Bertha Willie (see Figure 7b).

5a. Charley Haslem in Kelso Valley, 1936. He was quite old when this photograph was taken. Charley was a consultant for McCown, but Zigmond got no information from him. Some people regarded him as a curing shaman, while a few accused him of being a bewitching shaman; apparently, several attempts were made on his life.

b. Bob Rabbit was a widely-known weather shaman. 1937. He was also an eccentric and probably unreliable consultant. McCown worked with him.

6a. Setimo Girado, 1937. He was an important consultant for Zigmond; his wife Marie narrated myths to Cappannari; and two of their daughters were important consultants at a later time (see Figure 7a).

b. Gladys Nichols Girado in 1973. She also appears in Figure 1a.

7a. (l.-r.) Lida Girado and Clara Girado Williams, daughters of Setimo and Marie Girado, in 1973. Both were linguistic consultants for Zigmond, and Lida was the sole source of information for the linguist Curtis Booth. Clara translated narratives told by her mother to Cappannari.

  b. Bertha Willie Goings, daughter of Sam Willie, at Tehachapi in 1973. Bertha was especially helpful as a linguistic consultant.

8a. Martina Collins standing in front of a brush shade, 1936. She provided Zigmond with a few short narratives.

  b. Ramona Greene and her children in 1936 or 1937. Andy Greene (second from the left) was a helpful consultant for Zigmond.

9a. Marcelino Rivera and Isabella Gonzales at the Tejon Rancheria in 1937. They were the last survivors of the Kitanemuk tribe, and were brother and sister.

  b. (l.-r.) Maurice Zigmond and Stephen Cappannari at Dennisport, Cape Cod, in 1948.

10a. Johnnie Shoshone, Zigmond's Panamint consultant, standing on the ridge of the Panamint Range with Death Valley in the background.

  b. (l.-r.) Andy Shoshone and his grandfather, Panamint George, 1938. Andy translated his grandfather's narratives for Zigmond.

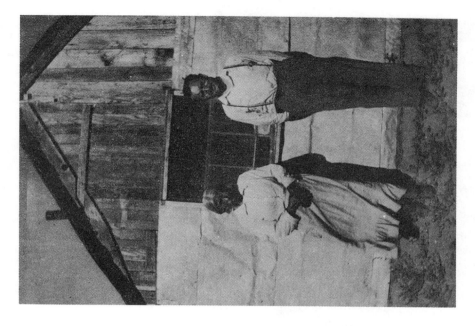

1. a. (l.-r.) Gladys Nichols, Lizzie Nichols, Emma Williams,
   Sophie Williams, and Elsie Williams, 1936.
   b. Emma Williams and Maurice Zigmond, 1936.

a

b

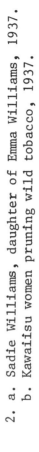

b

a

2. a. Sadie Williams, daughter of Emma Williams, 1937.
   b. Kawaiisu women pruning wild tobacco, 1937.

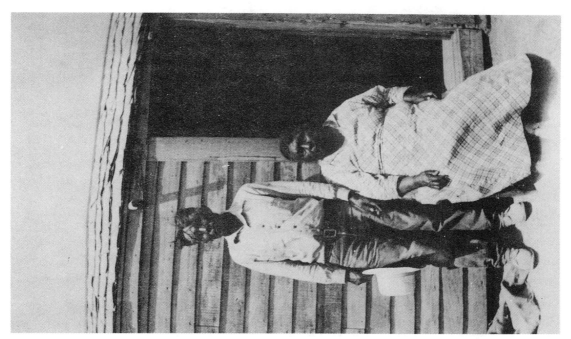

b

a

3. a. John Nichols with his hand in a mortar-hole, 1937.
   b. John and Louisa Marcus at home in Monolith, 1937.

4. a. Refugia Williams and daughters, 1937.
   b. Sam Willie and his family at Monolith, 1937.

b

a

a

b

5. a. Charley Haslem in Kelso Valley, 1936.
   b. Bob Rabbit, Kawaiisu weather shaman, 1936.

a

b

6. a. Setimo Girado, 1937.
   b. Gladys Nichols Girado, 1973.

a   b

7. a. (l.-r.) Lida Girado and Clara Girado Williams, 1973.
   b. Bertha Willie Goings at Tehachapi, 1973.

8. a. Martina Collins in front of brush shade, 1936.
   b. Ramona Greene and her children, 1936 or 1937.

b

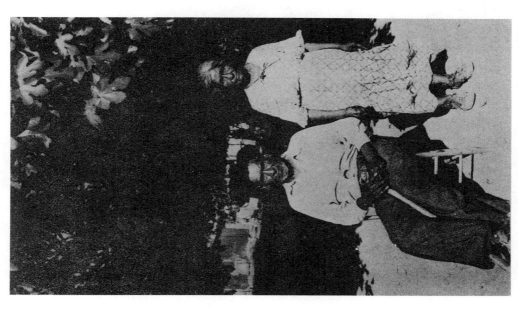

a

9. a. Marcelino Rivera and Isabelle Gonzales at Tejon, 1937.
   b. (l.-r.) Maurice Zigmond and Stephen Cappannari at Cape
   Cod, 1948.

b

a

10. a. Johnnie Shoshone on the ridge of the Panamint Range, 1938.
   b. Andy Shoshone and his grandfather, Panamint George, 1938.

Some other books available from Ballena Press: —

Heizer Robert F. (Selected and Edited by) FEDERAL CONCERN ABOUT CONDITIONS OF CALIFORNIA INDIANS 1853 to 1913: EIGHT DOCUMENTS. *Ballena Press Publications in Archaeology, Ethnology and History No. 13.* Beginning with the report of the first Superintendent of Indian Affairs for California, E.F. Beale, in 1852, the problems of establishing the five military reservations "for the protection of the Indians" in 1853 are then reviewed. In 1860 the Federal Government attempted termination for the first time in an effort to turn over to the State of California all Indian affairs in exchange for an annual appropriation of $50,000. The Senate considered, but rejected, the proposal in a lengthy debate which is recorded in the Congressional Globe.

Public outrage and pressure brought about official inquiries into the condition of Native Californians, and four such reports dating from 1874 to 1906 are reproduced here, including the John G. Ames and the Jackson-Kinney special agents reports on conditions among the Mission Indians of Southern California. The latter report was co-authored by Helen Hunt Jackson, the author of *Ramona.* That federal neglect continued is shown by two reports of C. E. Kelsey of 1904 and 1906. The final document is the address of President Wilson to the North American Indians of 1913. 152 pp., paper covers. 1979. ISBN 87919-084-1 $7.95

Merriam, C. Hart. INDIAN NAMES FOR PLANTS AND ANIMALS AMONG CALIFORNIAN AND OTHER WESTERN NORTH AMERICAN TRIBES. Assembled and Annotated by Robert F. Heizer. *Ballena Press Publications in Archaeology, Ethnology and History No. 14.* One of the major posthumous works to appear under the name of Merriam, this volume contains the Indian words in 122 languages for 417 plants (flowering plants, trees and shrubs) and animals (mammals, birds, reptiles, fish, insects, amphibians, etc.). Additional words together with annotations on folk beliefs about plants and animals, plants used in medicine or magic, etc., are in a separate section. The editor has added an introduction which puts the volume and its author in perspective, as well as two appendices: a select bibliography of the published writings of Merriam on California Indians. A fair prophecy is that this volume will be a standard reference source for all California ethnographers for the next century. 296 pp., maps, biblios., paper covers. 1979. ISBN 87919–085–X $12.95

Tuohy, Donald R. (Editor) SELECTED PAPERS FROM THE 14TH GREAT BASIN ANTHROPOLOGICAL CONFERENCE. *Ballena Press Publications in Archaeology, Ethnology and History No. 11.* Eight papers of substantial length covering four major subjects.

In archaeology Don D. Fowler reviews the several models applied as interpretive tools in Great Basin prehistory, and Emma Lou Davis reviews recent discoveries of early cultures at China Lake.

Physical anthropology is represented by Henry M. McHenry and Peter D. Schulz' survey of Harris Lines and dental hypoplasia evidence in prehistoric Central California skeletal materials and their implications for the prehistoric dietary regime.

Culture contact is treated by Robert N. Lynch on Indians and whites on western Nevada ranches; Richard O. Clemmer discusses piñon nuts and cattle in the Ely region; and Omer C. Stewart provides an important summary of federal relations with the Western Shoshone of Nevada 1863–1950.

Linguistics is represented by William H. Jacobsen's analysis of internal diversity and external relations of the Washo language, and by Pamela Munro's specialized paper on Chemehuevi.

171 pp., illus., maps, references, paper covers. 1978. ISBN 0-87919-077-9 $8.95

Send for free catalogue of complete list of books to: —
BALLENA PRESS
P.O. Box 1366
Socorro, New Mexico 87801
U.S.A.